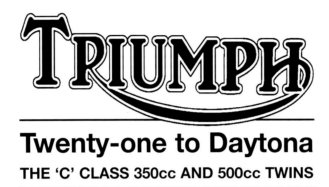

Twenty-one to Daytona
THE 'C' CLASS 350cc AND 500cc TWINS

Other Titles in the Crowood MotoClassic Series

Twenty-one to Daytona

THE 'C' CLASS 350cc AND 500cc TWINS

Matthew Vale

THE CROWOOD PRESS

First published in 2008 by
The Crowood Press Ltd
Ramsbury, Marlborough
Wiltshire SN8 2HR

www.crowood.com

British Library Cataloguing-in-Publication Data
A catalogue record for this book is available from the British Library.

ISBN 978 1 86126 997 3

Acknowledgements
This is my third book, and I would like to thank all those involved in its
preparation. These include my wife Julia and daughter Lizzie, who have put up
with me disappearing into the garage to work on the T100C or into the study
to write the book. Many thanks are due to Mick Walker, for providing me with
photos, and to Simon Cheney, who gave me some valuable insights into the
competition scene from the 1960s to the present day, and pictures and anecdotes
on the successful Cheney bikes. Finally I would like to thank Chris Goodburn,
Rowena Hoseason, Simon Smith and Jeff Cardew for putting up with me
badgering them for their anecdotes and pictures of their bikes.

Designed, typeset and edited by Focus Publishing,
Sevenoaks, Kent

Printed and bound in Singapore by Craft Print International Ltd

Contents

Introduction

Launched in 1957, the Triumph 'C' Series Twins started with the enclosed Twenty-one, so named to both mark the 21st anniversary of the formation of the Triumph Engineering Co., and as a measure in cubic inches of the capacity of the new bike. The bike was a 350cc unit construction twin, and was famous for its fully enclosed rear end. The Triumph 'C' Series soon grew to 500cc, and reused the famous Triumph 'Speed Twin' name in its earlier versions. In production until 1974, the 'C' Series twins were successful both commercially and in competition, winning the famous Daytona races in the USA in 1966 and 1967. The bikes still have an active following, and their small size, low weight and good spares availability make then as popular today as they were in their heyday.

Calling on the my own experiences, archive material, contemporary articles and road tests and current and past owners, this book looks at the development of the range, and charts this development through the many variants that were sold in the UK and abroad. The intention of the book is to provide information about all the variants of the range in one place, including the early Twenty-one and 5TA models. The book covers all the models produced, breaking them down into the touring models, the sporting road models, the high performance models and the offroad/competition models. The final Triumph model that used the 'C' series engine, the TR5T Adventurer/Trophy Trail, is also covered, as is the range's proposed replacement, the Triumph T35 Bandit. The book also explores ways to make the bikes more suitable and reliable for today's busy roads, and describes the full restoration of a US spec 1969 Trophy 500 T100C from a rolling wreck to factory fresh condition.

Matthew Vale, 2008

1 The Origins of the 'C' Class Twins

Triumph Motorcycles introduced their new 'C' Series range of vertical twins with the 350cc Twenty-one in 1957. The bike was powered by Triumph's first unit construction vertical twin engine, and while the cycle parts were conventional, the model's styling marked a major change, incorporating enclosure on a Triumph for the first time – indeed a first for any of the mainstream motorcycle manufactures of the time.

The new model was a softly tuned touring bike, which was in line with the policy adopted by most British factories at the time. It was standard practice to start with one or two softly tuned models, which would then be progressively developed to expand the range with more sporting versions. By introducing the 'soft' models first, the manufacturers were able to identify and fix any fundamental problems with the design which could be critical on models in a higher state of tune.

The 'C' range was to follow a typical development cycle. The range would gain more sporting models, such as the Tiger 90 350cc twin, and also grow in size to 500cc with the introduction of the 5TA Speed Twin – again, the first 500cc model being a softly tuned tourer. More 500cc sporting models followed; with on- and offroad competition models being produced as well as better roadsters. The model's most famous sporting success was winning the Daytona 200 races in the USA in 1966 and 1967, and the racing did improve the breed. The experiences of Triumph at Daytona resulted in major changes to the engine and frame of the range based on those

The first model in the 'C' Series Triumph range was the Twenty-one – the first postwar Triumph to incorporate enclosures.

As time went on, the Twenty-one lost its enclosure and acquired the classic Triumph style. Here is a Tiger 100 pictured at the Netley Marsh auto jumble in 2006.

made to the racers, personified in the Twin Carburettor T100R Daytona introduced for the 1967 model year. While the 350cc models were dropped in 1968, the 500cc models remained in production until the start of the infamous Meriden sit in at the end of 1973, culminating in the TR5T Trophy Trail/Adventurer. This model comprised a 500cc single carburettor engine fitted into a new BSA-derived offroad frame that carried its oil in the top tube.

Today, the 'C' Series twins continue to provide popular and enjoyable riding for many classic motorcyclists. The features that made the range popular when new are just as relevant to the current classic scene – the bikes have adequate performance, good handling, road holding and braking (in the later models at least) and are significantly lighter and more agile than the 650cc 'B' Range twins. In appearance the later models have the Triumph look, while the earlier models have a unique look of their own! The range today also benefits from good spares availability and a good range of knowledgeable specialists to help keep them on the road. All in all

the Triumph 'C' series bikes were and still are excellent middleweight machines, with many of the virtues and few of the vices of the larger twins from any of the British manufacturers.

A Brief History of Triumph

Triumph as a company started in 1885, set up by Siegfried Bettmann initially as an import-export company with interests in reselling pedal cycles and sewing machines. In 1887, Bettmann formed a partnership with Mauritz Johann Schulte, and the Triumph Cycle Co. started to manufacture its own pedal cycles in Coventry. The company started to manufacture their own motorcycles in 1902. During World War I, Triumph supplied some 30,000 motorbikes to the allied forces, and their performance and reliability gained them the nickname 'Trusty Triumph'. Post war, Triumph continued to expand and in 1923 started to produce motorcars as well as bikes. However, the 1930s depression put paid to many established companies, and in the mid-1930s the company was in trouble. Jack Sangster, then owner of Ariel,

The final model in the 'C' Series was the TR5T Adventurer/Trophy Trail. Produced in for 1973 and 1974 only, it used a BSA derived frame.

heard about Triumph's problems and bought the motorcycle part of the business, forming the Triumph Engineering Co. Ltd in 1936. As part of this takeover Sangster appointed Edward Turner, a talented young designer who worked for Sangster at Ariel, as chief designer and general manager. Sangster gave Edward Turner a relatively open hand, and this resulted in the autocratic Turner running Triumph almost as his personal fiefdom.

Edward Turner's first task on taking over was to revamp Triumph's range of somewhat lacklustre singles, which he achieved swiftly and competently, more than repaying Sangster's faith in him. Edward Turner restyled the 250cc, 350cc and 500cc singles in the existing range and named these new models the Tiger 70, 80 and 90 to reflect their notional top speeds.

The 'new' bikes were very well styled and popular, and gave a new lease of life to the company. Having got the company back on its feet, Edward Turner than pulled off the master stroke that moulded the future of Triumph, and arguably the whole British industry, by designing

Studio shot of Edward Turner – Triumph's autocratic leader from the 1930s through to the 1960s.

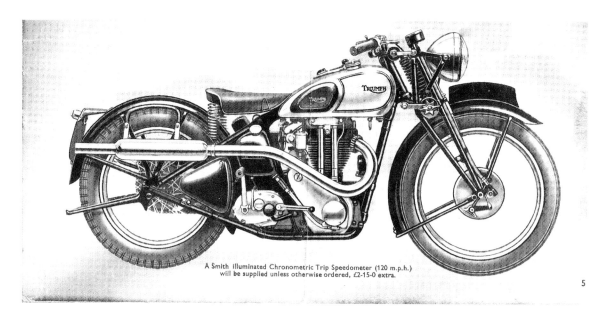

The 1939 Tiger 90 350cc single was typical of the range and shows Edward Turner's styling flair, which helped to revitalize the Triumph company.

The start of the line – the Speed Twin (5T) of 1939, a 500cc pre-unit vertical twin.

and getting into production the 500cc twin-cylinder Speed Twin. The new engine was slim enough to fit into the existing 500cc singles frame, and caused a real sensation when it was introduced to the market in July 1937.

At the start of World War II, Triumph's Coventry works turned to producing machines for the War Department, in the shape of the 3SW and 5SW, 350cc and 500cc side-valve singles. However, Edward Turner designed a 350cc twin, the 3TW, which was based on the civilian 3T engine, but with a three speed gearbox in unit with the engine. It was light and agile and in late 1940 the War Department passed it for production. Unfortunately, as the first pre-production batch of 50 machines was being prepared, fate intervened: on the night of 14 November 1940, the Luftwaffe blitzed Coventry and the Triumph factory was destroyed. Triumph was relocated to a temporary factory in Warwick while a purpose-built factory was prepared at Meriden. This facility opened in May 1942, and production resumed. However, it was not the 3TW 350cc twin that Meriden produced, rather a 350cc single, the 3HW, which was based on the pre-war overhead valve single cylinder model. Meriden also produced twin-cylinder engines based on the Speed Twin unit in the form of lightweight portable electric generators for the Army and the Royal Air Force.

At the end of the war, Triumph found itself with the most modern purpose-built motorcycle factory in the UK, equipped with many modern machine tools, and promptly reintroduced the 500cc Speed Twin and Tiger 100, alongside the 350cc 3H single and the new 350cc 3T twin. Triumph's markets were mainly overseas in the immediate post-war years, with Britain desperate to export goods to repay the debts incurred during the war, and this formed the basis for Triumph's success.

The US market was expanding rapidly, and Triumph pursued it with high-performance machines such as the Tiger 100. As demands from the US for ever more performance grew, the

After the war the T100 took up the performance mantle from the Speed Twin. Note the telescopic forks and the nacelle.

500cc engine was stretched to 650cc and the Thunderbird was introduced to the range.

During the 1950s Triumph was incredibly successful in the USA, with its unbeatable combination of performance and styling. Even though rivals such as BSA had a wider range of bikes, Triumph became the pre-eminent British make in the US, and, in turn, became increasingly reliant on that market. Despite BSA being Triumph's main rival in the USA (and the UK), it was not generally publicized at the time that in March 1951 Sangster sold Triumph to the BSA group, mainly to avoid paying punitive death duties. As part of the deal, Sangster became a director of BSA and eventually chairman in 1956. Edward Turner was made managing director of the BSA automotive division, which covered BSA, Triumph, Ariel, Sunbeam and New Hudson, as well as Daimler cars. Sangster retired in 1960, handing over his chairmanship to Eric Turner (no relation to Edward Turner). Edward Turner remained in his post as managing director until he retired in 1964.

Despite the merger, BSA and Triumph operated (and indeed competed) largely independently for many years with only limited co-operation on the design of the models in the separate ranges. While some components (such as brakes) were shared in the 1960s, and some 'badge engineering' was carried out, notably in the production of the TR25W Trophy model, closely based on the BSA B25 Starfire, the lack of co-operation between Meriden and Small Heath was exemplified by the rival Triumph Trident/BSA Rocket Three models.

These bikes were effectively two different models with only the engine layout in common. Both were 750cc triples, but rather than sharing major components, they had completely different frames and engine casings, thus losing many possible economies of scale in their production. The seeds of real co-operation only arrived in the 1971 model year, with a total revamp of the BSA and Triumph ranges. However, rather than fixing the bits that were broken, namely the old and outmoded engines across both the BSA and Triumph ranges, the management fixed the bits that were not broken, by replacing the frames and running gear of both the BSA and Triumph

In the 1960s BSA and Triumph were slowly bringing their model ranges together.
The Triumph TR25W was a 250cc single closely based on the BSA Starfire.

The rebuilt T100C featured in Chapter 6. In standard colours – Lincoln Green with a silver stripe on the top of the tank – the bike is as attractive in appearance as it is to ride.

650cc twin models and the unit singles range frames, while keeping the existing engines. Despite this piecemeal rationalization, the 'C' Series Triumph Twins continued with their old frame and running gear, only sharing ancillary parts such as switchgear and indicators with the rest of the range.

The revamp of the range, which cost a fortune, was intended to stem the decreases in profits which had hit the company in 1969 and 1970. It did not succeed in doing this, however, and BSA posted a massive loss of over £8 million in 1971. Things were little better in 1972, with losses of £3.3 million, and in 1973 the BSA name was dropped and the group was taken over by Norton Villiers, owned by Dennis Poore of Manganese Bronze Holdings. The new group, Norton Villiers Triumph, or NVT, proposed to close the Triumph plant at Meriden as a cost-cutting exercise, and relocate all production to the BSA Small Heath plant. This led to the Meriden workers barricading themselves in the plant in September 1973, in what became known as the Meriden Sit-In. No Triumphs were produced from this time until the end of the blockade, but the workers did release some batches of completed machines during the sit-in.

Eventually the workers were able to form a co-operative in March 1975, and production of Triumphs was restarted, but the plant only produced the 'B' Series 750cc twins, although a number of 1973-built 'C' Series 500cc Twins were released when the blockade was lifted. The co-operative limped on in Meriden until 1983, when the venture finally collapsed. The Triumph name and factory were bought by property developer John Bloor, who licensed production of the 750cc twin to Les Harris, who resumed manufacture from a factory in Devon for a few years in the late 1980s. Eventually Bloor resurrected Triumph with a completely new and up-to-date model range built in a new factory in Hinckley, Leicestershire, England in the 1990s, and these are Triumphs that can be bought today.

The Triumph Vertical Twin Legacy

When Edward Turner took over at Triumph in 1936, the range comprised the 250cc, 350cc and 500cc singles and a 650cc vertical twin designed by Val Page. Once he had livened up the singles, and stopped production of the twin, Turner was poised to stamp his mark on the British motorcycle industry. Taking his experience from Ariel in producing the Ariel Square Four, in 1937 he produced the first really successful version of the archetypical British motorcycle of the 1940s, 1950s and 1960s: the vertical twin. Rumoured to be based on half of the square four engine design, Edward Turner's design for the first Speed Twin was a 500cc twin cylinder engine that revolutionized British motorcycle design. The vertical twin engine, where the two cylinders were positioned side by side, was ideal for the times. It was compact enough to fit into the existing singles range frame and running gear with few changes, and looked like a twin port single – so did not scare off the more conservative customers while still attracting those who wanted innovation.

The configuration was almost as slim and light as a single, was cheaper to produce than a four or a V Twin, was smoother than a single thanks to its more manageable power impulses, was easier to start and in appearance was very similar to a twin-port single. The Speed Twin was arguably the first commercially successful vertical twin and all the other manufacturers were forced to follow suit and introduce their own vertical twins – but most had to wait until World War II was over before they could get their models to the market, giving Triumph a lead that they would not relinquish.

After World War II Triumph introduced a 350cc twin, the 3T, which was similar in layout to the 500cc Speed Twin but differed in detail. However, with demand for the 5T and the Speed Twin outstripping supply, the 3T was dropped in the 1951 to enable Triumph to concentrate on the more profitable 500cc and 650cc bikes. The range was to have no middleweight bike in it until the introduction of the Twenty-one in 1957.

Why the 'C' Class Twins?

The 350cc class was important in the UK in the late fifties, as it was considered to be the minimum size for a 'real' motorcycle that was capable of both weekly commuting and weekend touring. With some notable exceptions, such as Douglas's flat twins, the 350cc machines on the market in the 1950s were single-cylinder

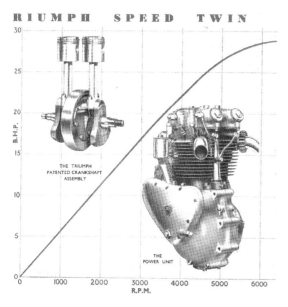

The 1939 Speed Twin engine defined the layout and the appearance of all subsequent Triumph vertical twin engines.

The Speed Twin's twin gear driven camshafts, separate rocker boxes, plunger oil pump and central flywheel crank were to be seen in all subsequent versions.

The BSA B31 was the definitive British 350cc bike of the 1940s and 1950s – a robust, versatile and reliable four-stroke single.

The Twenty-one was a modern design – unit construction for the engine and enclosure for the rear were in stark contrast to the then current bikes.

four-stroke machines, and most were based on, and used the running gear from, 500cc models. In addition, in the USA the 350cc capacity was seen as the right size for a starter bike.

The 1950s 350cc models from the mainstream manufacturers such as BSA, Ariel, Norton AJS and Matchless were heavy and relatively slow, but offered good reliability, steady usable perfor-mance and good handling and road holding. However, times were changing. While the gener-ic British 350cc single was a good machine, it did not offer much in the way of excitement and with the swinging sixties just around the corner, the time was right for a different take on the 350cc market. While Triumph could have resur-rected the pre-unit construction 3T or produced a sleeved-down Speed Twin to re-enter the 350cc market, the argument for a completely new model was compelling. The 350cc class was ready for a high performance middleweight, and Tri-umph needed a new range of engines. Edward Turner recognized this, and had besides a num-ber of other good reasons for the introduction of the Twenty-one.

The main British electrical component manufacturer, Lucas, was making noises about discontinuing the production of their expen-

The Italians knew how to style their machines – the 1958 Lambretta scooter was both stylish and practical.

TRIUMPH

The Best Motorcycle in the World

The 1958 Triumph brochure featured the then new Twenty-one on its cover, in a piece
of artwork that really sums up the spirit of the 1950s.

sive magnetos and DC dynamos, and was press-
ing motorcycle manufacturers to move over to
the AC alternator and coil ignition. The old
style of separate engine and gearbox was also
being superseded by unit construction, where
the engine, primary drive and gearbox were
housed in a single pair of castings which were
cheaper to produce than the separate casings
for the engine, gearbox and primary drive
needed previously. Edward Turner's Terrier and
Tiger Cub singles, first seen in 1952, had
shown the way for Triumph, and it was time to
up the game. Unit construction offered the
chance to produce a modern, compact power

unit that could be mounted in a new lightweight chassis. The combination of unit construction and AC alternator electrics would
lead to a light, compact and economical-to-
produce machine. Other advantages of unit
construction included fewer joints and a more
rigid structure, leading to (potentially) fewer
oil leaks, and fixed centres between the crank
and the gearbox, easing maintenance and keeping chains in line. The Twenty-one had all these
virtues and more. Finally, Turner also took the
opportunity to incorporate his latest ideas on
styling, with the introduction of the easy-to-
clean and smoothly styled bathtub.

Introduction of the Twenty-One

The Triumph Twenty-one was introduced in 1957, and was Edward Turner's attempt to produce a motorcycle that he thought the world was waiting for. The model name 'Twenty-one' had two facets; it celebrated the Triumph Engineering Company's 21st birthday in its current incarnation, and the capacity of the model – 350cc – is 21 cubic inches in the American capacity measuring scale. The styling of the Twenty-one, inspired by Edward Turner and executed by Jack Wickes, broke new ground for Triumph with its introduction of what became known as 'full enclosure'. The machine's looks were heavily influenced by the 1950s scooter boom, which popularized clean, enclosing bodywork, and by Edward Turner's own ideas of what a motorcyclist wanted; and of course it sported the completely new unit construction engine and gearbox.

The total enclosure of the rear half of the machine, a large, heavily valenced and styled front mudguard and the trademark Triumph nacelle produced a smooth-looking, easily cleaned motorcycle with only the new unit construction engine exposed to the elements and the gaze of the public. However, while the styling appealed to a proportion of the motorcycle-buying public (generally considered to be the more mature end of the market), the rear enclosure was quickly and accurately (but somewhat unkindly) nicknamed a 'bathtub' by the youth of the day as it resembled an upturned tin hip bath, while the large front mudguard was in turn nicknamed the 'Roman Helmet'.

Although the Twenty-one was the first all-new Triumph unit construction vertical twin, the engine design followed the well-proven layout of the 1937 Speed Twin with its gear-driven twin camshafts, and the overall appearance of the engine retained the pre-unit look with the distinctive Triumph timing case with the famous triangular timing cover with the small triangulate Patent plate in its centre. This approach to the engine's appearance contrasted with BSA's approach to unit construction with the A50 and A65 in 1962, where the engine was smoothly styled as a 'power egg' and bore no resemblance

The BSA A50 had its engine styled as a 'power egg' without the nod to the past that Triumph made with their new engine for the Twenty-one.

The WD Model T50WD

In the 1960s Triumph produced seventeen prototype models to compete for a large contract (some 3,000 machines) with the British Ministry of Defence.

These models had some unique features, such as a petrol tank modified to carry a 'snorkel' tube to feed air to the air cleaner from as high as possible, a special dirt- and dust-proof carburettor with a butterfly valve throttle operated by an external cable which was easy to change without dismantling the carburettor, and a 1950s front wheel and brake assembly with push-in front axle for easy front tyre changing.

However, the big contract for British MoD machines went to BSA for their WD B40 350cc single. Neil Shilton, in his book *A Million Miles Ago*, describes how Triumph were forced to put the tender price of their machines up by £30 'on instructions from the Chairman', thus ensuring that the BSA B40 won the contract – although, as the BSA machine was £30 cheaper than the Triumph even

before this, BSA would have won anyway. 'Price,' to quote Mr Shilton, 'was an important competitive factor'! So the 'C' Series Triumphs did not gain any significant orders from the MoD and thus was unable to build on the success of the NATO standard Triumph TRW 500cc pre-unit twin produced in the 1950s.

However, Triumph did sell 'militarized' unit construction Speed Twin models to, among others, the Dutch army during the 1960s, though these were broadly speaking standard T100/5TA models. One interesting feature was the 'snorkel' air intake, which ran under the fuel tank to emerge around the headstock, enabling the model to wade through deep water without ingesting it – whether the ignition system would have stood up to this sort of abuse is another matter. Note also the non standard carburettor – it is definitely not the special Amal developed for the BSA WD B40, but looks like a Zenith, a make with close association with Triumph.

The Dutch T50WD was close to standard, but had some unique features.

You can make out the snorkel arrangement for the air intake that runs through the petrol tank and exits in the nacelle, thus preventing the engine ingesting water when in deep water.

The butterfly valve carburettor is different from the Amal fitted to the contemporary BSA B40, and is believed to be a Zenith.

The Triumph Twenty-one was an attractive machine, and was considered to be bang up to date when it was introduced.

externally to the A7/A10 unit despite sharing the overall layout of the earlier engine.

The finish of the Twenty-one for its introduction to the press was a metallic silver grey, which was applied to the whole the machine, including the frame – indeed the adverts in the press at the time were illustrated with machines with frames painted in the same colour as the rest of the bike.

However, Triumph must have realized that this overall silver finish would not be practical, and production machines were finished with black frames, with the bath tub, fuel tank, nacelle, fork sliders and mudguards finished in Shell Blue (or 'Polychromatic Azure Blue' to quote the US magazine Motorcyclist) – a very light blue/silver metallic colour which was attractive, and gave the

The Triumph range marketed in the USA for 1960 comprised the 200cc Cub, the 350cc and 500cc 'C' Series unit twins, and the 650cc pre-unit twins.

Triumph was awarded the Queen's Award for Industry in 1967, due mainly to their success in exporting bikes to the USA.

Twenty-one a lightness of appearance that effectively disguised the extent of the bodywork, which could have looked quite bulky in the wrong colour.

In service and under review from road tests at the time, the Twenty-one received pretty much unanimous praise for its appearance and practicality. The model formed the basis of a range that would remain in production until 1974. It was also destined to win on of the USA's most important races – the Daytona 200, and to help Triumph to win the Queen's Award to Industry in 1967, based mainly on the company's success in exporting bikes to the US.

2 Model Development

This chapter looks at each of the models that made up the 'C' Series twins. Like most of the product lines of the major British manufacturers at the time, the 'C' Series range grew and expanded throughout the 1960s, with many different models of both 350cc and 500cc; though with Triumph's demise in the 1970s it shrank back to just two models.

Broadly speaking, the models can be divided up into three types of use – namely touring, on-road sports and offroad sports; and into two capacity ranges, 350cc and 500cc. There were only two 350cc machines in the range – the original softly tuned Twenty-one/3TA and the sporting Tiger 90. Introduced as the first model in the range in 1957, the 3TA lasted until 1966, and when it was dropped there was no real replacement, as the 350cc tourer market had disappeared. In contrast the T90 was introduced in 1963 to serve the small sports market, and

remained in the range until 1968, when it was quietly dropped – again a victim of the declining market for 350cc machines.

The first 500cc bike in the range was the touring 5TA, introduced in 1959. While it was virtually identical to the Twenty-one, with bathtub and nacelle, the 5TA was painted all over, including the frame and forks, in Triumph's trademark Amaranth Red, linking it to the pre-unit Speed Twin that was so successful in the 1940s and 1950s. The softly tuned 5TA lasted until 1966, when its role as the tourer in the range was taken over by the T100.

The road-oriented (as opposed to the offroad variants) Tiger 100 entered the range in 1960, and was the sportster of the range. However, the 1960 model really hid its lights under a bushel, as it still had the bathtub and nacelle of the Twenty-one. When the US market got the pared-down TR5A/R (for Road) in 1961, the bathtub-

Here is a late 3TA pictured at Shepton Mallet Show, 2006. Note the bikini – an abbreviated version of the bathtub enclosure.

equipped T100/A was sold alongside it. The T100 slowly improved on the styling front, with the introduction of the Bikini rear enclosure and separate headlamp for 1962, and complete loss of the enclosure in 1963. The model inherited the mantle of tourer rather than sportster in 1967 when the Daytona T100R was introduced, and was finally dropped from the range at the end of the 1970 model year.

The 500cc T100T (UK) or T100R (US) Daytona was introduced in 1967, and with its twin carburettors took over from the T100 as the 'top of the range' sportster. The Daytona remained in production until the 1974 model year, with actual production ceasing in September 1973.

The offroad models had almost as confusing names as the road models. The offroad or Competition models were all 500cc variants, were never fitted with enclosures or the nacelle, and were usually distinguished from the road based models by their smaller-capacity fuel tanks and upswept exhaust systems. Aimed mainly at the US export market, the first offroader was the 1961 TR5/C. Then 1962 brought the first 'C' model, the T100S/C, which still sported a low-level exhaust system; the famous upswept high-level exhaust eventually appeared for 1963.

The T100 competition model ran on until the end of the 1972 model year, and it was replaced by the TR5T Adventurer / Trophy Trail in 1973, production of which finished in 1974.

In this chapter references are made to the timing and drive sides when describing the various elements of a 'C' Series Triumph. The timing side (the side with the valve drive gears) is the right-hand side of the bike, and the drive side (the side with the chains) is the left-hand side – both assuming the rider is sitting on the bike.

TOP: *The 5TA was the first development of the Twenty-one. This model, pictured in 2007, is pretty original, and is still in its Amaranth Red finish – including the frame.*

MIDDLE: *The T100SS was the sporting model of the range from 1960 until the introduction of the Daytona in 1967.*

BOTTOM: *Almost the last year of production of the twin-carburettor Daytona, this is a 1973 model.*

The 350cc 3TA Twenty-one (1957–66)

The Twenty-one was the father of the range, and was introduced in February 1957 to an appreciative audience. The softly tuned 350 quickly established itself as a popular and reliable tourer and commuter, even if it did not hit the mark with Triumph's more enthusiastic sporting fans. The major feature of the model was its styling. The rear enclosure, large enveloping front mudguard and nacelle made for a clean, modern and unique design. The bike's reasonable performance, easily cleaned enclosure and excellent mud guarding appealed to the more mature rider.

As was the way with Triumph, the development of the specific model was somewhat limited, as resources were spent on producing larger and more sporting versions. Indeed, the Twenty-one's engine had no major revisions to its tune throughout its life, and when it was deleted from the range in 1966, it still made 18.5bhp. Still, during its production life, the overall package gained from the developments made to the other models in the range. On its introduction the model had a black frame and chromed wheel rims, while the tinware (tank, bathtub, nacelle and front mudguard) was finished in Shell Blue. One notable feature was the under-seat layout. The Twenty-one had a large rubber tray extending back from the battery along to the rear frame loop, which had indentations to accept the tools supplied with the model – rather than having them scrunched up into a bag. The seat was hinged on its left-hand side, and when opened gave access to the tool tray, oil tank and battery. There was even some rudimentary security offered – the knob used to release the seat could be unscrewed and removed, affording some protection from the light-fingered!

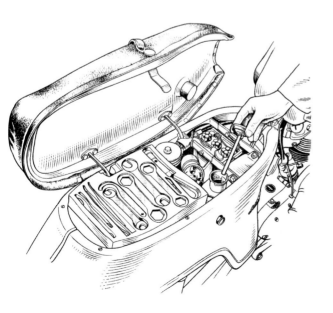

TOP: *Although an export model, some T100Cs escaped to be sold in the UK. Here is Rowena Hoseason's example, with the trademark high-level exhaust system.*

MIDDLE: *The Twenty-one was a ride-to-work bike, or tourer – softly tuned and easy to ride, with the benefit of excellent weather protection.*

BOTTOM: *The under-seat layout of the 21 was neat, with a rubber tray to hold the tools.*

First and Last Twenty-one/3TA Specifications

	1958 Twenty-one	1966 Twenty-one (3TA)
Engine		
Bore and stroke	58.25mm × 65.5mm	58.25mm × 65.5mm
Capacity	348cc	348cc
Compression ratio	7.5:1	7.5:1
Power	18.5bhp at 6,500rpm	18.5bhp at 6,500rpm
Carburettor		
Type	Amal Monobloc	Amal Monobloc
Specification	375/25	375/62
Number	1	1
Transmission		
Engine sprocket (teeth)	26	26
Clutch sprocket (teeth)	58	58
Gearbox sprocket (teeth)	18	17
Rear sprocket (teeth)	43	46
RPM at 10mph in top gear	760	808
Gear ratios		
Top	5.31	6.04
Third	6.3	7.36
Second	9.32	9.71
First	13.00	14.96
Wheels and tyres		
Front	325 × 17	325 × 18
Rear	325 × 17	350 × 18
Front Brake	7in (18cm) single leading shoe	7in (18cm) single leading shoe
Rear Brake	7in (18cm) single leading shoe	7in (18cm) single leading shoe
Dimensions		
Seat height	28½in (72.4cm)	30in (76.2cm)
Wheelbase	51¼in (131.4cm)	53½in (136cm)
Length	80in (203cm)	83¼in (211.5cm)
Width	26in (66cm)	27in (68.5cm)
Ground clearance	5in (12.7cm)	6in (15.2cm)
Weight	340lb (154.4kg)	341lb (154.7kg)
Fuel capacity	3½ US gal (16ltr)	3 UK gal (13.5ltr)
Oil capacity	5 pints (2.8ltr)	6 pints (3.35ltr)

The Opposition – the Norton Navigator

The only other British 350cc four-stroke twin marketed in the 1960s was Norton's Navigator. This bike, a direct competitor of the Triumph Twenty-one, was introduced in 1961, and was a development of the Jubilee, a 250cc twin. The Navigator had a 350cc unit construction engine which was housed in a composite pressed steel and tubular construction frame, which was based on a Francis-Barnett item – a fellow member of the Associated Motor Cycles (AMC) group. Unlike the Jubilee, the Navigator was equipped with the famous Norton 'Roadholder' front forks, and also had the 8in (20cm) front brakes and the alloy hub from the larger Nortons.

The Navigator was available in two versions – the Standard and De-Luxe. The De-Luxe mirrored the Twenty-one in having full enclosure of the rear end – similar in coverage to the Twenty-one, but not nearly as stylish. The enclosure was more angular than the organic shape used by Triumph, though the angular shape and styling lines pressed in did allow for some attractive two-tone paint jobs.

The De-Luxe Navigator performed much the same as the Twenty-one, with a top speed of around the mid-80s mph (130s km/h) given in contemporary road tests in favourable conditions. A practical and comfortable top speed was considered to be around the 70mph mark (113km/h).

The Navigator was supplemented by the Electra 400 in January 1963. This model was aimed at the US market, and was equipped with an electric start (the Lucas M3 unit, mounted on the top of the primary chain case) and indicators. The bike also had a 12v electrical system, following the then current practice of having two 6v batteries mounted in series in an enlarged under-seat carrier. The Electra also gained the 7in (18cm) rear brake and alloy hub from the larger bikes in the Norton range.

The Navigator only remained in production from 1961 through to the autumn of 1965, and the Electra was dropped at the same time. All in all the bikes were not a success, with general complaints of oil leaks, less than perfect mechanical reliability and poor electrical components. They never received the development work they really needed and represent a sorry end to what could have been a class leading bike.

The 350cc Norton Navigator De-Luxe featured enclosure and mudguarding very similar in style and function to the 3TA and 5TA.

Feature	Norton Navigator De-Luxe	Triumph Twenty-one (3TA)
Bore and stroke	63mm × 56mm	58.25mm × 65.5mm
Capacity	349cc	348cc
Compression ratio	8.5:1	7.5:1
Front brake	8in (20cm)	7in (18cm)
Rear brake	7in (18cm)	7in (18cm)
Wheelbase	51½in (130.8cm)	52¾in (134cm)
Seat height	29in (73.6cm)	29¼in (74.5cm)
Length	81in (206cm)	81in (206cm)
Width	Not stated	26in (66cm)
Ground clearance	5½in (14cm)	5in (12.7cm)
Weight	335lb (152.2kg)	340lb (154.5kg)
Power	Not stated	18.5bhp at 6,500rpm

The Standard Navigator was styled in the traditional Norton manner, which many people found understated in comparison to the Triumph 'naked' machines.

The Navigator's big brother, the 400cc Norton Electra, can still be seen on the road. This one was spotted at the 2007 Fleet Lions run.

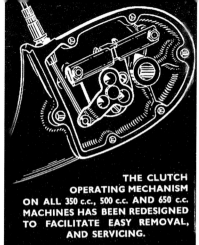

THE CLUTCH OPERATING MECHANISM ON ALL 350 c.c., 500 c.c. AND 650 c.c. MACHINES HAS BEEN REDESIGNED TO FACILITATE EASY REMOVAL, AND SERVICING.

LEFT: There still some bikes around with the original under-seat layout with its rubber tray for the tools – this example was spotted at Netley March in 2006. RIGHT: A revised clutch mechanism was introduced in 1964 across the range.

The first changes to the range came mid-season in 1957, when the fuel tank gained fixings for the parcel grid common to the rest of the range, and the frame gained lugs for a prop stand and for luggage rack and pannier mounting. The rubber under-seat tray was discontinued from 1959 – there were some issues with the tray filling with water and rusting the tools. The arrangement reverted back to the tools being stored in the traditional tool roll, which was stored under the seat in a small tray.

The next change to the range was the renaming of the model from Twenty-one to 3TA in September 1958, coincidently at the time of the introduction of the 500cc 5TA. However, just to keep the punter confused, Triumph continued to use the 'Twenty-one' name alongside 3TA!

For 1960, the excellent Triumph quickly detachable rear wheel became an option. For the 1961 season the bike gained a primary chain tensioner, which comprised a rubber coated steel blade. This was fixed to the lower alternator stud, and had a screw driven adjuster rod, accessed via a plug in the bottom of the chain case cover. Importantly the steering head angle was steepened by 2 degrees to 65 degrees. This change was driven by the US market, where the sportier models were beginning to make a name for themselves off road, and the new angle gave better control off road.

For 1962, the main change was the introduction of an optional colour – Silver Bronze for the tank, bathtub and front mudguard. There were no significant changes for 1963, as development was concentrated on the more sporting models in the range.

The 3TA lost the bathtub in 1964 when it acquired the smaller bikini. The nacelle and 'Roman helmet' front mudguard were retained.

The final 3TA only retained the nacelle – the bathtub, bikini and 'Roman helmet' front mudguard were all lost.

The next significant change to the 3TA came in 1964, when the fully enclosed bathtub was swapped for a much smaller enclosure, quickly nicknamed the 'bikini'. This abbreviated enclosure ran from the front of the bike's midriff back to the rear suspension top mounts, leaving the rear wheel exposed. A new rear mudguard was needed, and the whole bike looked slimmer and sleeker than before. The forks were updated, with thicker stanchions and external springs, but on the 3TA the nacelle was retained. Mechanically, there was a new clutch operating mechanism, and the distributor was lost, with the contact breaker points being relocated in the timing case, driven directly from the exhaust camshaft. Lucas 4CA points were specified, with a separate set for each cylinder.

The tank, bikini, mudguards, nacelle and front fork lower legs were finished in a metallic light brown finish called Silver Beige.

By 1965 sales of the 3TA were declining, but the changes that were made across the rest of the range were nevertheless incorporated, presumably to assist in production rationalization. These included modifying the frame to incorporate a bolted-on bracing strut from the steering head to the top of the seat tube. This meant that the fuel tank was no longer a stressed member, so it could be rubber mounted at four points, but lost capacity as it had a tunnel incorporated to clear the new top frame member. The Tiger 90's cylinder head was adopted, along with the smaller diameter (1¼in rather than the previous 1½in) exhaust pipes, and the large 'fireman's helmet' front mudguard was replaced with the blade type used on the other non-enclosed machines in the range, with the standard Triumph three hooped stays fixing it onto the forks, which also acted as a braces for the forks. The final year for the 3TA was 1966, when the machines lost all of their rear panelling, resulting in an exposed oil tank of 6 pints' capacity on the timing side and a new matching side panel on the drive side. The frame was modified again, with the new bracing strut from the headstock to the rear of the front loop now brazed on rather than bolted, and the electrics became 12 volt, with a solid state Zener diode at last providing reliable voltage control.

The Twenty-one/3TA was dropped from the range during 1966, just as the model gained alloy con rods to replace the steel ones previously fitted. The 350cc market had almost disappeared in the UK by then, and the model had in fact disappeared from the Triumph range in the US by 1961. The 3TA was not replaced; softly tuned commuter/touring bikes were not wanted by the increasingly youth-driven market.

ABOVE: A 5TA prototype with a glass-fibre bathtub. The experiment was not successful, and production models were equipped with steel bathtubs.

BELOW: The 1959 Triumph brochure artwork features the new 500cc Speed Twin – the transfer of a revered name onto a completely new bike.

Middleweight Tourer: The 500cc 5TA Speed Twin (1959–66)

Introduced in September 1958, the middleweight tourer 5TA Speed Twin reintroduced a famous name after the dropping of the 500cc pre-unit twin of the same name. The 5TA was to all intents and purposes a bored-out version of the Twenty-one. It's frame and running gear was identical to the Twenty-one in all but finish, with all tinware, frame and running gear painted in Triumph's trademark colour Amaranth Red, in a successful attempt to link the new Speed Twin with its pre-unit ancestor.

The engine was in the same state of tune as the 3TA, with the same camshafts, and sharing an identical compression ratio of 7.5:1, but with new head, pistons and barrel the 490cc engine pushed out 27bhp – up by a significant 8.5bhp on the Twenty-one's 18.5bhp. This was a 45 per cent power increase for a 42 per cent increase in capacity. The important

First and Last 5TA Specifications

	1959 Speed Twin (5TA)	1966 Speed Twin (5TA)
Engine		
Bore and stroke	69mm × 65.5mm	69mm × 65.5mm
Capacity	490cc	490cc
Compression ratio	7:1	7:1
Power	27bhp at 6,500rpm	27bhp at 6,500rpm
Carburettor		
Type	Amal Monobloc	Amal Monobloc
Specification	375/3	375/35
Number	1	1
Transmission		
Engine sprocket (teeth)	26	26
Clutch sprocket (teeth)	58	58
Gearbox sprocket (teeth)	20	19
Rear sprocket (teeth)	43	46
RPM at 10mph in top gear	670	723
Gear ratios		
Top	4.80	5.4
Third	5.62	6.6
Second	8.35	8.7
First	11.56	13.4
Wheels and tyres		
Front	325 × 17	325 × 18
Rear	325 × 17	350 × 18
Front brake	7in (18cm) single leading shoe	7in (18cm) single leading shoe
Rear brake	7in (18cm) single leading shoe	7in (18cm) single leading shoe
Dimensions		
Seat height	28½in (72.4cm)	30in (76.2cm)
Wheelbase	51.75in (131.4cm)	53½in (136cm)
Length	80in (203cm)	83¼in (211.5cm)
Width	26in (66cm)	27in (68.5cm)
Ground clearance	5in (12.7cm)	6in (15.2cm)
Weight	350lb (159kg)	341lb (154.7kg)
Fuel capacity	3½ UK gal (16ltr)	3 UK gal (13.5ltr)
Oil capacity	5 pints (2.8ltr)	6 pints (3.35ltr)

CLOCKWISE, FROM TOP LEFT:

Close-up of the glass fibre bathtub on the 1958 5TA prototype.

The 5TA engine was virtually identical to the 3TA's.

The 5TA retained the distributor to drive the contact breakers and send the sparks to the plugs.

The under-seat layout of the 5TA was neat. Note the removable pull knob, and in this model there's a tool tray and Boyer electronic ignition box.

Paul Webb's Speed Twin – this bike was not typical of the sort of British bike available in the early 1980s, being reasonably original and retaining its tinware.

thing was that the weight of the two models also remained very close, with the 5TA at 350lb (159kg) being only 10lb (4.5kg) heavier than the 3TA's 340lb (154.4kg). Hence the power-to-weight ratio of the 5TA was substantially better than that of the 3TA, giving much better performance. The prototype 5TA was produced with a glass-fibre bathtub, but this were not a success and was replaced with pressed steel items for production.

As a tourer, the 5TA was a pleasant and under-stressed machine with a reasonable performance. The bike was reliable, and its appearance and development broadly followed that of the 3TA. That is to say there were minor changes that were usually introduced as a result of the development of the sportier T100, which was in demand in the US market.

The 5TA actually had very few significant changes made to it, which indicates that the bike was pretty much right on its introduction. The problem was that, like with the Twenty-one, the 'mature tourer' market that the 5TA was aimed at was not as buoyant as the new youth market, with its promise of ever-increasing sales.

For the 1960 season the bike remained much the same as in the previous year, but it did gain a slipper-type primary chain tensioner, which was needed as the extra power of the 500cc engine stretched the 'pre-stretched' chain significantly and at a greater rate than the Twenty-one could manage. The bike was finished overall (the frame and tinware) in Ruby Red, a brighter shade of the previous year's Amaranth Red.

For 1961, as with the Twenty-one, the foam tool tray was replaced by a new tool roll kept in a new small steel tray under the seat. The frame's steering head angle was increased from 65 to 67 degrees. Few changes were made for 1962 and 1963 – mainly a slight alteration to the overall colour, 1963 models being painted in Cherry Red.

The 1964 models were changed rather more than in preceding years. The full bathtub was replaced by the bikini, and the distributor was replaced by Lucas 4CA points in their own compartment under a chrome cover in the timing case.

Heavyweight forks with external springs replaced the earlier more flimsy design, the

The 5TA lost its bathtub and sported the bikini enclosure and narrow front mudguard for 1965.

nacelle carried a magnetic Smiths speedometer replacing the chronometric item fitted in previous years and the finish reverted to a more conventional scheme, with gloss black for the frame nacelle and fuel tank top, and silver sheen bikini, mudguards, fork legs and fuel tank bottom.

The model gained a new, slimmer front mudguard for 1965, and the new four-point fixing, rubber-mounted fuel tank. The final Speed Twins were produced in 1966. They lost the bikini completely, sporting T100-style exposed oil tank and matching side panel, but retained the nacelle. Paintwork remained the same as on the 1964 model.

The Speed Twin had come to the end of its life, in effect superseded by the T100SS, which in turn was to lose its crown as Triumph's super sports middleweight to the twin carburettor Daytona in 1967. The world had moved on, and there was no place for a cooking 500cc twin which cost just as much to produce as a sports model but had to be sold for less.

Speed Twin 500 c.c.

The final 5TA of 1966 had lost all its enclosures, with the exception of the nacelle.

Electric Start – What Happened?

As I was writing this book, I uncovered two vague references to a prototype 'C' range engine equipped with an electric start. Roy Bacon, in *Triumph Twins and Triples* (see Bibliography), makes a passing reference: 'For police use the 350 was also available with an electric starter fitted to the front of the crankcase and driving through the timing gear.'

And David Gaylin and Lindsay Brooke, in their volume Triumph Motorcycles in America (see Bibliography), also referenced this feature: 'Triumph had revealed an electric starter-equipped Speed Twin at the 1960 Earls Court Show, but it was aimed at British police bikes only'.

Advice from fellow author David Gaylin indicated that a prototype Lucas M3 starter-equipped 350cc Twenty-one model was displayed at the 1960 London Earls Court Motorcycle Show, and he pointed me towards the 17 November 1960 edition of *Motor Cycling*. This issue of the magazine is the 'Show Number' for the 1960 Earls Court Golden Jubilee London Cycle and Motor Cycle Show. Each exhibitor had a short write-up of their offerings, and under Triumph the writer says:

'A pointer to future trends is seen in a radio-equipped "Twenty-one" which incorporates the M3

Lucas electric starting operating from a 12v system.'

This brief description was accompanied by a sketch showing the starter motor mounted ahead of the engine in the old pre-unit dynamo position. An extended timing cover accommodated the drive end of the starter, while its body extended into a hole made in the front engine plates. Otherwise no other details were forthcoming from the press of the day. The brochures of the time made no mention of the existence of an electric start model, and the detailed specification sheets that Triumph issued in the 1960s to detail the changes made from standard to police-specification machines also had no mention of an electric start either as standard or as an option.

A trip to the London Motorcycle Museum a couple of days after uncovering the above resulted in me being somewhat surprised to see the timing side crankcase of a 'C' Series twin with an extended timing side cover and a Lucas electric starter attached to it. As can be seen from the pictures, the front timing case has been extended to accommodate an additional gear wheel, which engaged with the exhaust camshaft gear wheel. The new gear wheel was connected to the Lucas electric starter

The 5TA electric start prototype timing-side crankcase, showing the fitting of the starter motor in the front engine plates.

through a sprag clutch, which is missing from this example. The starter motor fitted very neatly into the front engine plates, and the outer timing cover was extended forwards to cover the works.

Triumph was no stranger to electric starting, as the Tigress Scooter (TW2S) had been equipped with just such a device since 1958, and in some ways it is strange that they did not pursue this option on the 'C' Series twins, especially in the later 1960s when the Japanese threat was increasing. Norton had proved the concept with their Electra model – a 400cc develop-

ment of the 350cc Navigator, which had an electric starter as standard in 1963.

The Norton's starter operated through the primary drive, and was not such a neat design as the Triumph – but at least it made it into production!

However, although aimed at the American market, the Norton did not sell, so perhaps Triumph was not wrong in not going to market with an electric-start 'C' Series twin. It was a shame, as the Triumph design was a very neat job, and why Triumph never put it into production must remain a mystery!

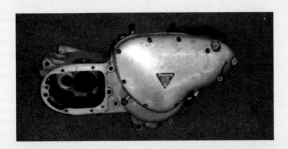

TOP LEFT: *The timing side of the crankcase half, showing the extended timing cover that fits over the end of the starter motor. The starter would turn over the engine via the exhaust camshaft drive through the gear train to the crankshaft pinion.*

TOP RIGHT: *Top view of the crankcase half, showing the connection between the starter motor and the timing chest.*

ABOVE: *The electric start crankcase with the Lucas starter clearly visible sandwiched between the engine plates and bolted into the timing case.*

The Norton Electra actually made it into production in 1963, and was aimed mainly at the US market.

A Sporting 350: The Tiger 90 (1963–8)

The Tiger 90 was the only 350cc derivative of the original Twenty-one/3TA range. It was conceived as a sporting 350cc and was introduced in October 1962 at the Paris show for the 1963 season. In appearance and specification the bike was similar to the T100SS, with bikini, separate chromed 7in headlamp with ammeter, the T100 front forks, still with internal springs, and slim sports mudguards in steel.

It featured a separate speedometer and (optional) tachometer mounted on the top yoke from the start, aiding its sporting appearance. For the model's introduction the finish was quite striking, with the tank, bikini and mudguards painted Alaskan White – it may not have been practical but certainly looked good. The frame and other parts were in gloss black. The Tiger 90 engine unit was tuned to the same specification as the T100SS,

with identical camshafts and a 9:1 compression ratio. The T90 unit always had its Lucas 4CA contact breaker points in the timing cover, and was fitted initially with a siamesed exhaust system with the silencer on the timing side. The engine gave 27bhp at 7,500rpm, which gave the bike a brisk performance with a top speed of over 90mph (145km/h), and acceleration to match. The downside of this was that the power was stacked up in the higher rev band, and the bike needed revving to extract maximum performance. A single Lucas PRS8 switch for ignition and lights was placed on the drive-side bikini, just below the seat nose. The peppy performance and generic Triumph styling soon caused the T90 to be nicknamed the 'Baby Bonnie'.

The Tiger 90 lost its bikini in 1964, when it gained a new drive-side panel that matched the oil tank. The drive-side panel carried two new Lucas rotary switches (type 88SA) for lights and ignition. The side panels were finished in black,

The Tiger 90 was introduced in a pleasant all-white colour scheme in 1963. There are still a surprising number about – this model was pictured in 2006 at Kempton Park.

The T90 lost its bikini in 1964, and was styled like the 650cc Bonneville, with black oil tank and matching side panel.

the mudguards in white with a gold stripe, and the fuel tank was painted in gold and Alaskan White. The front forks were changed for the heavyweight, outside spring types, and the siamesed exhaust system was dropped in favour of separate pipes and silencers. A new design of pushrod tubes with improved seals attempted to stop leaks from these troublesome items. The gearbox gained needle roller bearings for the lay shaft, and the speedometer and tachometer were changed to Smiths Magnetic types from the previous chronometrics.

The main change to the T90 in 1965 was the adoption of the modified frame with steering head brace, and a Pacific Blue and silver tank and silver mudguards.

For 1966 the T90 got 12v electrics, with Zener diode voltage control. The diode was mounted behind the left-hand side panel, which was not ideal for heat dissipation. The side panel still carried the

For 1965, the T90 had a new frame and paint job.

First and Last Tiger 90 Specifications

	1963 Tiger 90 (T90)	1968 Tiger 90 (T90)
Engine		
Bore and stroke	58.25mm × 65.5mm	58.25mm × 65.5mm
Capacity	349cc	349cc
Compression ratio	9:1	9:1
Power	27bhp at 6,500rpm	27bhp at 6,500rpm
Carburettor		
Type	Amal Monobloc	Amal Concentric
Specification	376/300	R624/2
Number	1	1
Transmission		
Engine sprocket (teeth)	26	26
Clutch sprocket (teeth)	58	58
Gearbox sprocket (teeth)	17	17
Rear sprocket (teeth)	46	46
RPM at 10mph (16km/h) in top gear	810	808
Gear ratios		
Top	6.04	6.04
Third	7.15	7.36
Second	9.80	9.71
First	14.67	14.96
Wheels and tyres		
Front	325 × 18	325 × 18
Rear	350 × 18	350 × 18
Front brake	7in (18cm) single leading shoe	7in (18cm) single leading shoe
Rear brake	7in (18cm) single leading shoe	7in (18cm) single leading shoe
Dimensions		
Seat height	30in (76.2cm)	30in (76.2cm)
Wheelbase	53½in (136cm)	53½in (136cm)
Length	82¼in (209cm)	83¼in (211.5cm)
Width	26½in (67.3cm)	26½in (67.3cm)
Ground clearance	7½in (19cm)	6in (15.2cm)
Weight	336lb (152.8kg)	337lb (152.8kg)
Fuel capacity	3 UK gal (13.5ltr)	3 UK gal (13.5ltr)
Oil capacity	5 pints (2.8ltr)	6 pints (3.35ltr)

The 1967 T90 was close to the end of the line, but retained its attractive looks.

separate ignition and light switches, and a Yale-type cylinder ignition switch with a proper Yale key was introduced. The engine gained the alloy connecting rods previously used on the T100. The colours were changed to Grenadier Red and Alaskan White, and this was the year of the infamous light grey handle-bar grips, which soon showed the dirt but are today sought-after items for the serious restorer.

For 1967, development on the mechanicals had largely ceased, but the T90 did gain the new frame as used by the T100T, and the light switch migrated upwards to the headlamp shell, behind the ammeter. The yearly revamp of colours gave it a hi-fi scarlet top and white underside to the fuel tank, black side panel and oil tank and white mudguards.

For 1968, the Tiger 90 had modified front forks as per the T100, and the colours were Riv-iera Blue on the fuel tank's top with silver below. Mudguards were painted silver. The T90 was discontinued in October 1968, by which time the 350cc class was pretty much dead – the models offering little performance gains over the newer 250cc models (especially from Japan), but costing as much to tax and insure as a 500cc model.

The Sporting Road 500s: Tiger T100A and T100S/S (UK) T100/A, T100A/R, T100SR and T100R (US) (1960–70)

Triumph's first performance model in the range was the 500cc T100A (or T100/A) Tiger 100 of 1960. The bike was equipped with a tuned engine, with high compression pistons (9:1) and

The first sporting 500cc bike in the range certainly did not look like a sports model. With its nacelle and bathtub, the T100A was not a Triumph of sporting styling.

First, Middle and Last Tiger 100 Specifications

	1960 Tiger 100 (T100A)	1966 Tiger 100 (T100S/S)	1970 Tiger 100 (T100S)
Engine			
Bore and stroke	69mm × 65.5mm	69mm × 65.5mm	69mm × 65.5mm
Capacity	490cc	490cc	490cc
Compression ratio	9:1	9:1	9:1
Power	32bhp at 7,000rpm	34bhp at 7,000rpm	n/a
Carburettor			
Type	Amal Monobloc	Amal Monobloc	Amal Concentric
Specification	375/35	375/273	R626
Number	1	1	1
Transmission			
Engine sprocket (teeth)	26	26	26
Clutch sprocket (teeth)	58	58	58
Gearbox sprocket (teeth)	20	18	18
Rear sprocket (teeth)	43	46	46
RPM at 10mph (16km/h) in top gear	670	763	763
Gear ratios			
Top	4.80	5.70	5.70
Third	5.69	6.95	6.95
Second	8.44	9.18	9.18
First	11.66	14.09	14.09
Wheels and tyres			
Front	325 × 17	3.25 × 18	3.25 × 18
Rear	350 × 17	350 × 18	350 × 18
Front brake	7in (18cm) single leading shoe	7in (18cm) single leading shoe	7in (18cm) twin leading shoe
Rear brake	7in (18cm) single leading shoe	7in (18cm) single leading shoe	7in (18cm) single leading shoe
Dimensions			
Seat height	29¼in (74.5cm)	30in (76.2cm)	31½in (80.1cm)
Wheelbase	51¾in / 131.4 cm	53½in (136cm)	53½in (136cm)
Length	80in (203cm)	83¼in (211.5cm)	83¼in (211.5cm)
Width	26in (66cm)	26½in (67.3cm)	26½in (67.3cm)
Ground clearance	5in (12.7cm)	6in (15.2cm)	6in (15.2cm)
Weight	363 ld / 165 kg	337 ld / 152.8 kg	352 ld / 161 kg
Fuel capacity	3½ UK gal (16ltr)	3 UK gal (13.5ltr)	3 UK gal (13.5ltr)
Oil capacity	5 pints (2.8ltr)	6 pints (3.35ltr)	6 pints (3.35ltr)

While it may not have looked sporting, the T100A was a performance machine. Here is Dennis Dicker racing a T100A at the 1962 Thruxton 500-mile production race.

revised camshafts, giving 32bhp against the 27bhp of the Speed Twin. Another major change for the T100A was the introduction of Lucas Energy Transfer ignition, which powered the ignition coils directly from the alternator, enabling the bike to run without a battery. However, and possibly unfortunately for a sports model, the T100A's running gear and styling was the same as the Speed Twin's, complete with bathtub, nacelle and large front mudguard. The fuel tank top was painted gloss black, and the underside was finished in ivory. The rest of bike, including the frame, was finished in gloss black.

With high bars the bike was introduced to the US market – where the punters quickly relieved the bike of the extraneous tinware!

Despite the bike being styled like the touring 5TA, the T100A had a brisk and respectable performance, and was pretty soon pressed into production racing. The bikes looked incongruous with their bathtub and heavy front mudguard but achieved some success in the role.

For 1961 Triumph continued to produce the T100A with bathtub, roman helmet front mudguard and nacelle for the UK market, but the power had risen to 34bhp. The Energy Transfer

The T100A sported a full set of tinware – bathtub, nacelle and 'Roman helmet' front mudguard.

The 1961 TR5A/R for the US market was styled more in keeping with its sports performance.

The 1962 T100SS at last gave the British market some sports styling – albeit with bikini, but a separate chromed headlamp replaced the staid nacelle.

In 1962 the US models did not even have the bikini. These set the scene for classic Triumph styling through the 1960s.

ignition system was dropped during the 1961 model year, with the model reverting to the battery and coil system from frame number H22430.

For the US market, Triumph had heeded to the cries of the Triumph dealers for more sporting styling, and produced the TR5A/R, a sporting roadster, with separate chromed headlamp, slim mudguards and no enclosure. In fact the factory went so far as to have no side panel on the left-hand side, leaving the battery and air filter open to the elements. The model had a bracing strut bolted between the steering head and the seat nose, which needed a new 2½ gal fuel tank with a tunnel to accommodate it. This is a rare model, with only 350 being built. The US market tank was finished in Kingfisher Blue, while the UK specification tank was black and silver.

When the UK 1962 season came round, Triumph at last relented on the enclosure question and the Tiger 100S/S was introduced. The naming of this model is varied in the Triumph literature – it was T100S/R or T100R for the US and T100S/S or just plain T100S in the UK for various years. To the general public, the model was known as the T100SS – the name that defined the sporting single-carburettor 500cc twin. This model still produced 34bhp at

7,000rpm, but had the bathtub replaced by bikini, the nacelle replace by a separate chrome headlamp, and the Roman helmet design replaced a slim painted blade-type front mudguard. The bike weighed in at 336lb (152.8kg) as opposed to the previous year's 363lb (165kg) so performance was enhanced, and the looks were exactly what the public were looking for. The fuel tank of the UK market T100SS was finished in Kingfisher Blue top and Silver sheen lowers.

This model set the scene for the evolution of the T100SS sports machine – and it was to be evolution not revolution. Over the next eight years, the model's appearance would not change much, apart from the colour scheme. However, there were significant engineering modifications made over the period, so while superficially the T100SS appeared to be stagnating, this was not the case.

Nonetheless, the UK T100SS saw little change for 1962 and 1963, apart from new silencers. The US T100S/R (Sports/Road) model lost its bikini in 1962 and never looked back, showing the UK models the way to go. For 1962 the UK model tank was painted Regal Purple with Silver lowers, while the bikini was painted Kingfisher Blue. For 1963 the UK model tank was Regal Purple and silver, and the bikini was silver.

The Opposition: The BSA A50

When Triumph designed the 'C' Series twins they started off with the 350cc 3TA and then enlarged it to produce the 500cc models. While the running gear was perfectly adequate, the overall dimensions of the range were those of a smaller bike. In fact the 'C' range has always been popular with smaller persons because of this. In contrast BSA's 1960s A50 500cc twin shared its basis with the 650cc A65 – and so used bigger and stronger components that could take the extra power of the 650cc engines. The immediate effect of these two different design philosophies can be seen by comparing the specifications of a mid-1960s A50 and T100 – both single-carburettor touring bikes.

As can be seen from the figures below, the A50 is significantly larger than the T100 – not surprising considering the 650cc genes in its make-up. However, the extra size and weight do impact on the bike's performance, especially the extra 71lb (32kg) in weight – a 21 per cent increase over the T100. There is also a major difference in price, with the Triumph costing a massive £30 more than the BSA. In 1968 this represented an average of around two weeks' wages of a typical blue-collar worker.

While there were sports derivatives of the A50, notably the US-market Cyclone, the A50 Star and Royal Star in the UK was always sold as a tourer, and never gained the twin

carburettor head, racing camshafts and high compression cylinder head of the Cyclone. The model was always in the shadow of its 650cc companions in the BSA range, and was also under attack from lower down the BSA range with the 441cc BSA Victor singles. While contemporary road tests found that A50 made a pleasant tourer, it really did nothing outstanding, and was hampered by its weight and bulk in a market that was moving away from solid ride to work or touring mounts and heading off down the hedonistic youth trail, with performance and appearance overtaking practicality.

The performance figures put the Triumph ahead, but not by a large margin. In fact, when the figures are analysed, it is possible to see the two markets that the bikes are aiming at – broadly speaking, 'Youth' and 'Maturity'. The Triumph has a sporting image, backed up by the victories at Daytona, and the light, manageable bike is aimed at the youth market. The BSA by contrast is aimed squarely at the more mature members of the motorcycling fraternity – it is a 'sensible' bike. The BSA is just a bit staid but offers a big bike for small money, with the only real trade-off being the lack of performance, which, although probably not that significant in the real world, would be enough to deter the youth market.

Component	BSA A50 Royal Star	Triumph T100SS
Wheelbase	56in (142cm)	53½in (136cm)
Seat height	32in (81cm)	30in (76.2cm)
Length	85in (216cm)	83¼in (211.5cm)
Width	28in (71cm)	26½in (67.3cm)
Ground clearance	8in (20cm)	6in (15cm)
Weight	408lb (185kg)	337lb (152.8kg)
Power	Not stated	34bhp at 7,000rpm
Bore and Stroke	65.5mm × 74mm	69mm × 65.5mm
Capacity	499cc	490cc
Price (March 1968)	£315	£345

Feature	BSA A50 Royal Star	Triumph (1963 Model T100 SR)
Top speed	97mph (156km/h)	100 (161km/h)
Acceleration 0–30mph	3.4 seconds	2.5 seconds
Acceleration 0–60mph	8.5 seconds	8.0 seconds
Acceleration 0–80mph	14.0 seconds	14.0 seconds

The A50 certainly retained the BSA corporate look, with its chromed fuel tank and bright red paintwork.

The UK-specification bikes were more sensible than the US variants, with larger fuel tanks and larger mudguards.

The BSA A50 was a derivative of the 650cc A65, and as such was a big and heavy bike in comparison to the T100.

Mouth Organ, Eyebrow and Picture Frame

Over the life of the 'C' Series twins, the Triumph styling was a definitive influence on the range, providing a mix of controversy and acceptance probably in equal parts. The all-new enclosure of the first models provided the controversy, while the traditional sleek functional styling of the late 1960s and early 1970s models virtually defined what a good-looking motorcycle should look like. The range exhibited cutting edge ideas on the styling of motor cycles, and part of the overall styling was the fuel tank badge. Triumph tank badges are now styling icons and have played a major role in defining the marque. In the 1960s it was common to see Rockers exhibiting their loyalty to Triumph with belt buckles made from the iconic tank badges.

There has been some confusion over the nicknames given to the Triumph tank badges over the years. There are four main types used from the 1950s onwards. The first one comprised four flutes or bars with the Triumph name superimposed on top. This design does not seem to have a nickname given to it.

In 1957 Triumph introduced a new tank badge across the range, the famous 'mouth organ' design. This badge carried the Triumph 'sweeping R' logo over a square cross-hatched pattern that looked like the mouthpiece of a mouth organ – hence the name.

This badge remained in use for nine years, lasting until the end of the1965 model year, when a new design arrived for 1966. With Triumph's advertising literature exhorting the punter to 'Go Modern Go Triumph', the new tank badge was a much cleaner and modern design. It had the Triumph 'sweeping R' logo forming the bottom of the badge, with a flute running across the top and additional fluting on the leading edge. The design was vaguely eye-shaped and was rapidly nicknamed the 'eyebrow'.

However, the 'eyebrow' design did not last very long, and was replaced with a cleaned-up design in 1969. This design has the Triumph logo superimposed on a rectangular box, with a chrome flute above it tapering into a point at the forward edge. This design was christened the 'picture frame' – for the obvious reason that the Triumph logo was framed by the rest of the badge.

The 'picture frame' tank badge remained in use almost until the end of Triumph production at Meriden. The badge was used up to 1981, when a plain 'Triumph' Sweeping R replaced it as the tank badge on the 2gal US tank used on the T140 Bonneville.

FAR LEFT: *The 'four bar' tank badge was largely superseded by the time the 'C' Series was introduced, but did appear on some early US-market offroad TR5s.*

LEFT: *The 'mouth organ' tank badge was so called because of the square hatching behind the Triumph 'sweeping R' logo.*

The 'eyebrow' tank badge looked a bit like an eye, and was cleaner and less cluttered than the mouth organ.

The 'picture frame' tank badge framed the Triumph 'sweeping R' logo in a box, and was simpler and cleaner than the 'eyebrow'.

In the UK it took until 1964 for the T100S/S to lose its bikini. While this did not give any decrease in weight, the new side panel and matching oil tank, along with slim mudguards, gave the bike a much more sporting look, reflecting the styling of the 650cc Bonneville. This made the UK bikes much more appealing to the youth market, and gave more commonality between the UK and the US models. New front forks, similar to those fitted to the 650cc models, gave improved damping, and the push rod tubes received the latest modifications to attempt to make them oil tight. The fuel tank was Hi-Fi Scarlet top and silver lowers, and the oil tank and side panel from now on were painted gloss black.

For 1965, the T100S/S was not changed too much, with a new tank fixing method and with a bolt-on top tube bracing strut. This meant a new petrol tank, with a tunnel to accommodate the bracing strut, and a new four-bolt rubber mounting method. Fuel tank colours were Burnished Gold uppers and Alaskan White lowers.

Another new frame was adopted in 1966, this time with the previous year's bolt-on bracing strut braised into new cast lugs to provide a one-piece front loop. A new wider swinging arm was also fitted, giving room for a larger section rear tyre – although this was aimed more at the offroad models. Fuel tank colours were Sherbourne Green uppers and Alaskan White lowers.

Significant changes were made to the T100SS for 1967, with the adoption of the new cylinder head, which incorporated the lessons learned from the 1966 Daytona race winner. However, this model did not appear in the US – only the T100C and Daytona were marketed in that important market. Most significant was the last incarnation of the frame, with another new front loop, which had a large-diameter top tube with a smaller-diameter bracing strut running under it to brace the headstock. A new fuel tank, with a three-point rubber mounting system (one bolt at the back and two at the front) was introduced with the new frame. The T100S/S was now effectively superseded as the main sports 500cc by the T100T Daytona, with its twin carburettors and racer-derived name. Fuel tank colours were Pacific Blue uppers and Alaskan White lowers.

In 1968 the T100S/S was now taking second place to the Daytona, but still benefited from developments made to the range. It was equipped with the new shuttle valve two-way damped forks, and adopted the new Daytona-type cylinder head, with its larger ($1\frac{17}{32}$in) diameter inlet valve and 39-degree valve angle. The carburettor was now a 26mm Amal Concentric. The primary chain case was equipped with the cover that allowed timing by strobe, and the contact breaker points were the new Lucas 6CA type, which allowed each cylinder to be timed individually. Fuel tank colours were Aquamarine (metallic blue) uppers and silver lowers.

Development of the T100S/S for the UK market continued in 1969, and it benefited from the new timing-side ball main bearing combined with the end feed crank. This was the last major engine modification made to the range and resulted in a virtually bullet-proof bottom end. The front brake was replaced by a twin leading shoe 7in unit in a new full width hub on all but the very first models produced that year. The factory was moving over to specifying Unified thread forms that year, but while some components were converted, others were not. Fuel tank colours were Lincoln Green uppers and silver lowers.

The last year of the T100S was 1970, when the bike gained the new breathing system that helped to cut down on oil leaks, but otherwise remained much the same as in 1969. The fuel tank colour was Jacaranda Purple.

The Competition 500s (1960–71)

While the 'competition' models of the 'C' Series range are, in some people's opinion, the most attractive and versatile models in the range, they

A 1970 T100SS at a period petrol station.

were never officially listed as being available to the UK market, and in fact do not appear in any UK market brochures. The majority of them were shipped out to the USA, where they formed the basis of many a racing career. The competition potential for the 500cc unit twins was realized early, and the first 'official' sports models were listed in 1961, aimed at the American market.

Based firmly on the cycle parts and engine of the T100A, the TR5A/R and TR5A/C were competition-oriented machines, and featured the styling cues that would come to epitomize Triumph's sporting machines through the 1960s – separate chromed headlamp with clock(s) mounted above on the top yoke, slim front mudguard, gaitered front forks and no 'streamlining' enclosures – in fact, on introduction the models did not even have a cover on the left-hand side to conceal the battery. Both bikes had 6in-diameter (15cm) headlamps, and the brochures of the time show the models with low-level, sometimes siamese exhaust systems,

which must have been somewhat impractical for offroad use. The mudguards were painted silver, and the fuel tank was Kingfisher Blue on top with silver below. The oil tank was gloss black. The models started the 1961 model year with the Energy Transfer ignition system, but as with the T100A the system was dropped mid way through the 1961 model year, with the model reverting to the battery and coil system from frame number H21122.

For 1962 the models were superseded, with the road-oriented TR5A/R becoming the T100S/R Tiger Road Sports (see previous section), and the offroad TR5A/C becoming the T100S/C Triumph Enduro Trophy. These both benefited from the improvements made to the other models in the range, and the T100S/C gained a smaller fuel tank and offroad tyres as standard, and a black headlamp shell. The most significant change was to the frame, where a strengthening strut was bolted from the steering head to the frame top tube. This meant the fuel tank was no longer a stressed unit, and the frame was stiffer, and was the first in

A 1970 T100SS in its natural environment – on the road.

a series of modifications to bring the handling and road holding of the whole range up the standards of the opposition. The new smaller tank was secured using a strap that ran from front to back. The 1962 brochure shows the T100S/R equipped with a tachometer (rev-counter) driven from the timing side of the exhaust camshaft through a modified timing cover. The colour scheme was the same as in 1961.

The models were further developed in 1963, losing the distributor and repositioning the points in the timing cover, driven directly from the exhaust camshaft. At last the exhaust pipe on the offroad model was upswept, running on the drive side of the machine into a single silencer. Alloy mudguards replaced the heavy steel units fitted hitherto.

The model range remained largely unchanged for 1964, and for 1965, when the fuel tank colour was changed to Burnished Gold top with Alaskan White lower.

For 1966 the T100S/C was renamed the T100C, and the fuel tank colours were Sherbourne Green upper and Alaskan White lower. For 1967, the T100C's most significant change was the introduction of the new frame, with the

The first of the competition models was the TR5A/C of 1960. This was a US-market model.

The TR5 was renamed T100 for 1962 – this is a 1962 T100SC Enduro Trophy.

The T100S/C evolved slowly, and was an effective offroad competition machine. This is a 1965 model.

The T100S/C marketing was relatively low key, but made the point that it was 'The top choice for Woods, Enduro and club competition'.

stronger headstock casting and permanently brazed top tube replacing the previous bolt-on unit, which, with a revised lower top tube, provided a proper triangulation of the headstock. The model also gained a new upswept exhaust system, with two separate silencers at waist height on the drive side, and stainless steel mudguards. The bike also at last gained a side panel on the drive side, and a chromed 6in (15cm) headlamp. The fuel tank was coloured Pacific Blue upper and plain white lower.

For 1968 the T100C gained small individual chromed heat shields on the front exhaust pipes, and the fuel tank was painted entirely in Hi-Fi Aquamarine (a metallic dark greeny-blue) with polished stainless steel mudguards. The model name was changed to Trophy 500 to reflect the model's sporting prowess.

The 1969 models at last gained a decent front brake, with a full width 7in (18cm) twin leading shoe item being fitted. The new TLS brake needed a new front hub, with a spoke flange on the

The 1967 T100C now sported practical stainless steel mudguards and two silencers to meet ever more stringent noise legislation.

First, Middle and Last Tiger 100C Specifications

	1963 Tiger 100 (T100C)	1967 Tiger Competition (T100C)	1971 Trophy 500SS (T100C)
Engine			
Bore and stroke	69mm × 65.5mm	69mm × 65.5mm	69mm × 65.5mm
Capacity	490cc	490cc	490cc
Compression ratio	9:1	9:1	9:1
Power	38bhp at 7,000rpm (straight through exhaust)	38bhp at 7,000rpm	38bhp at 7,000rpm
Carburettor			
Type	Amal Monobloc	Amal Monobloc	Amal Concentric
Specification	376/273	375/273	R626
Number	1	1	1
Transmission			
Engine sprocket (teeth)	26	26	26
Clutch sprocket (teeth)	58	58	58
Gearbox sprocket (teeth)	18	18	18
Rear sprocket (teeth)	46	46	46
RPM at 10mph (16km/h) in top gear	740	744	744
Gear ratios			
Top	5.70	5.70	5.70
Third	6.75	7.8	6.97
Second	9.26	11.25	9.16
First	13.86	18.1	14.1
Wheels and tyres			
Front	3.25 × 19	3.50 × 19	3.25 × 19
Rear	4.00 × 18	4.00 × 18	4.00 × 18
Front brake	7in (18cm) single leading shoe	7in (18cm) single leading shoe	7in (18cm) twin leading shoe
Rear brake	7in (18cm) single leading shoe	7in (18cm) single leading shoe	7in (18cm) single leading shoe
Dimensions			
Seat height	30in (76.2cm)	30in (76.2cm)	30in (76cm)
Wheelbase	53½in (136cm)	53½in (136cm)	53½in (136cm)
Length	84¼in (213.9cm)	83¼in (211.5cm)	83in (211cm)
Width	26½in (67.3cm)	27in (68.5cm)	27in (69cm)
Ground clearance	7½in (19cm)	7½in (19cm)	7½in (19cm)
Weight	336lb (152.8kg)	336lb (152.8kg)	342lb (155kg)
Fuel capacity	3½ UK gal (16ltr)	2¾ UK gal (10.8ltr)	2¼ UK gal (10.2ltr)
Oil capacity	5 pints (2.8ltr)	6 pints (3.4ltr)	6 pints (3.4ltr)

ABOVE: *Factory shot of the 1968 T100C shows the twin silencers, solid heat shield for the rider and the lack of any protection for the pillion's legs!*

BELOW: *The 1969 T100C was given the glamour treatment by Triumph in their brochure. Note the 7in (18cm) flanged front hub, which carried the twin leading shoe front brake.*

OPPOSITE: *The author's 1969 T100C shows off its bare timing side. Note the oil pressure warning light switch on the front of the timing cover and the non-standard indicators.*

brake side to allow the braking area to run up to the edge of the hub.

The hub was slightly wider than the previous straight-spoke design, which meant that wider front fork yokes were used. The new front brake was introduced some months into the production run, the first 1969 models (up to engine frame number XC07583 – and including the T100C restored for this book) having the 1968 front end.

The fuel tank was painted Lincoln Green, with a silver stripe down the centre of the tank, with the join between the two colours lined in gold. A notable change was the 'chip basket' heat shied on the exhaust that gave protection to the pillion passenger's legs at long last!

Few changes were made for 1970, the most noticeable being the rather striking Jacaranda Purple paint used on the fuel tank – a dark metallic purple.

While 1971 saw the introduction of new frames, forks and running gear for the 650cc models, the T100C for 1971 retained last year's frame, forks and wheels.

The main changes were peripheral to the overall machine, using the new corporate handlebar switches, indicators and 'gargoyle'-style rear lights. The headlamp ears gained rubber mounts for the headlamp, and the stainless steel mudguards were retained, with the rear very truncated as a style feature.

The fuel tank was painted in Olympic Flame with Black scallops above the picture frame tank badge.

Although not listed in most of the publicity brochures, the 1972 T100C continued much as the 1971 model, the only major change being the switch to 'push in' exhaust pipes; the fuel tank colour also changed to a top cover of Cherry Red with Cold White lowers, and gold lining between the colours. No tank 'knee' rubbers were fitted.

The T100C was not listed for the 1973 model year, and the on/offroad mantle was taken over for the 1973 model year by the TR5T Trophy Trail/Adventurer.

Close-up detail of the 1969 'chip basket' or 'barbecue grill' heat shield.

The 1970 T100C – probably the best styled and most attractive of the T100 line.

The exhaust system on the T100C was its main styling point. The exhaust pipes were curved sinuously around the front of the engine as shown on this 1971 T100C.

The 1971 T100C was a great-looking bike. Fitted with indicators as standard, the bike was good on- or offroad.

LEFT: *The bare timing side of the T100C emphasizes the light and lithe styling of the competition models. This is a 1971 T100C.*

OPPOSITE: *In 1971 the Triumph brochures went from artistic to moody with this shot of the US-spec T100C on the beach.*

TRIUMPH

500 cm³ Trophy 500

Building on Success – The 500cc T100T, T100R Daytona (1967–74)

The only 'C' Series unit twin that sported twin carburettors as standard was the Daytona model, so named because of Triumph's success at the Daytona races in the USA in 1966 and 1967. Introduced for the 1967 model year, the Daytona T100R effectively took over the sports role in the range previously taken by the T100S/S. The T100S/S for 1967 was the effective replacement for the 5TA, which was discontinued in 1966, although it should be noted that there were only two 500cc models marketed in the US for 1967 – the T100R Daytona Super Sports and the T100C Sports Tiger – Triumph's naming conventions being largely devoid of any real logic! The Daytona built on the development work that gave Triumph victory at the US's National Championship Road Race held at Daytona in Florida, and the most obvious visual change from the T100SS was the introduction of twin Amal 376/324/5 Monobloc carburettors.

The frame was new, and was based on the Daytona racers. While it was still of brazed lug construction with a separate bolt-on rear sub-frame, it sported a revised thicker top tube and headstock with a new steering head angle of 62 degrees (down from the previous year's 65 degrees), and also featured the triangular plates on the rear sub-frame that supported and stiffened the ends of the swinging-arm pivot. The engine boasted a new cylinder head with a shallower combustion chamber and no squish band, and the valve angle was reduced – that is, the valves were more vertical.

The the inlet valve diameter was increased in size to 1^{17}_{32}in to improve breathing through the new twin carburettors. New cams were fitted, with a profile based on the current Bonneville specification, the famous E3134 profile, and larger radius tappet feet were fitted to minimize wear and improve valve opening performance. Claimed engine power was 39bhp at 7,400rpm, in contrast to the T100S/S output of 34bhp at 7,000rpm. The compression ration remained the same as the T100S/S at 9:1. However, the engine still retained the timing side bush and the associated oil feed via the bush to the big ends.

To add to the punters' confusion over Triumph's 1960s model naming, the 1967 Daytona

The Daytona was introduced in 1957 as the new contender for the 500cc sports roadster.

The 1968 Daytona was attractive in green and white. Note the use of
the flanged hub and the large 8in (20cm) single leading shoe brake.

The Opposition – the Honda 450 'Black Bomber'

The Japanese industry was gearing up in the 1960s to challenge the US and European makers – especially the British. The Japanese had initially entered the UK and US market in the late 1950s with small-capacity bikes, but as the 1960s progressed, larger-capacity bikes were introduced. Probably the most significant of these was the Honda CB450 – a 444cc twin aimed directly at the sports 500s produced by the British manufacturers. It was nicknamed 'Black Bomber' at the time because of its standard black and chrome finish and the fact that it went like a bomb – that is, it was quick, not that the engine exploded! The bike was much better specified that its British counterparts, with chain-driven double overhead cams, torsion bar valve springs, 8in (20cm) twin leading shoe front brake, and electric start. The motor produced a claimed 43bhp at 8,500rpm and was reliable and oil-tight, although a *Motorcycle Mechanics* test (March 1968) did point out that:

> There are routine jobs of maintenance on the sportster which the average owner might find difficult, such as 'tappet' and carburettor adjustment and ignition timing. To get these spot on a rider could well have to have the bike serviced by his local Honda dealer and this could increase the general running costs.

But the article does go on to say that this was the price you have to pay for having so much power from such a sophisticated mid-range machine. Performance of the Black Bomber was considered by *Motorcycle Mechanics* to be brilliant for the capacity – giving a 0–60 time of 7.5 seconds and a maximum speed of 104mph (167km/h); and braking performance was also excellent, with a braking distance of 28ft 6in from 30mph (8.7m from 48km/h).

However, if you compare the bike with a 1967 T100R Daytona, tested by *Cycle World*, an interesting picture emerges.

Comparing the specifications of the two bikes, while the Honda produces 2bhp more than the Triumph (roughly 5 per cent) the Honda weighs a significant 72lb (33kg) more (roughly 21 per cent). Hence it is not that surprising that the Triumph outperforms the Honda – indeed, what is surprising is that the Triumph's performance margin over the Honda is not greater. Another factor in the relative popularity of the bikes is the price – the Honda costing £20 (approximately 6 per cent) more, and £20 in 1968 was a significant sum.

Where the Honda really did score was in its refinement and reliability. Despite the comments made above about getting the bike serviced at a Honda dealer, a well-serviced and maintained CB450 could be run

Feature	Honda Black Bomber	Triumph Daytona T100R
Top speed	104mph (167km/h)	105mph (169km/h)
Acceleration 0–30mph	2.0 seconds	3.4 seconds
Acceleration 0–60mph	7.5 seconds	7.0 seconds
Acceleration 0–100mph	25 seconds	21.3 seconds
Standing start ¼ mile	15.8 seconds	14.9 seconds
Standing start ¼ mile terminal speed	88mph (142km/h)	90mph (145km/h)

The performance of the Triumph is consistently higher than that of the Honda – but not by very much, and the two bikes would probably be pretty much equal on the road.

Feature	Honda Black Bomber	Triumph Daytona T100R
Weight	412lb (187kg)	340lb (154kg)
Power	43bhp at 8,500rpm	41bhp at 7,200rpm
Capacity	444cc	490cc
Bore and stroke	70mm × 57.8mm	69mm × 65.5mm
Price (March 1968)	£365	£345 (T100T)

The Honda CB450 'Black Bomber' was sophisticated, but performance wise was very evenly matched to the T100R Daytona.

hard and long. Oil leaks were the exception rather than the rule and the level of equipment (electric start, indicators, reliable electrics, decent switchgear and so on) would take some years to appear (if at all) on the British opposition. Still, sales were slow in the UK so Honda tarted up old stock in 1968 by painting the tank and side panels red, fitting dropped handlebars and fitting a chromed headlamp to make a 'Sport' model. *Motorcycle Mechanics* pointed this out at the time, and justifiably moaned about the poor quality of these modifications.

The new paint was badly 'orange peeled' and the chrome headlamp was happily rusting away after some 180 miles (290km) of use by the magazine.

While the Honda has a reputation for sophistication and high performance, the facts only support the sophistication side. Perhaps the most significant issue is the survival rate of the respective machines. In a recent and popular classic bike meet in the UK (2007) that I attended, the Fleet Lions Run, out of the 150 or so bikes attending there were fifteen to twenty 'C' Series Triumphs and one Honda CB450.

The Daytona styling did not change much over the years of manufacture: as this 1968 model shows, why change a good thing?

was supplied in the same colour scheme as the T100S/S, Pacific Blue and white, and even carried the script 'Tiger 100' on the side panel.

For 1968 the Daytona remained largely unchanged, but the previous year's Amal Monobloc carburettors were replaced with the new Amal Concentric, in 1 1/8in choke size, and the con rods were beefed up. An 8in (20cm) diameter single leading shoe front brake replaced the previous 7in (18cm) unit. The paint scheme remained the same as the T100C – Aquamarine and silver.

There were significant engine changes for 1969, which was also the year that any significant new development of the model really ceased – probably in anticipation of T35 Fury project that was scheduled for release in 1971. The major change for 1969 was the introduc-

The 1969 Daytona was given the same glamour treatment as the T100C.

It's 1969, and a Daytona hides from the photographer in a field! Triumph's advertising sometimes did it no favours.

tion of the 'end-feed' crank, where the oil feed to the big ends went through a drilling in the end of the timing side of the crank. The crank itself was still a one-piece forged unit with bolt on flywheel, and was supported on the timing side by a ball bearing – the timing side bush at long last being pensioned off. This modification reflected the changes made for the Daytona racers, and made the engine pretty much bullet-proof. A new timing case was needed, incorporating the oil feed, and provision was also made for a oil pressure warning light at the front of the case. Both the camshafts were changed to the famous E3134 racing form and were nitrated as standard to cut down wear.

However, the Daytona name did appear on the drive-side side panel – with a flowing script 'Daytona Super Sports' on the UK models, and a more plain 'Daytona' on the US market models. The rolling chassis benefited from the 8in

(20cm) twin leading shoe brake that was also fitted to the 650cc twins, and the front fork yokes were slightly wider to accommodate the new hub and brake assembly. The tank colour was Lincoln Green and white.

The model had detail changes made for 1970, including changes to the engine breather, allowing the engine to breathe directly into the primary chain case. The model colour was Jacaranda Purple and silver – a startlingly garish hue that certainly was in keeping with the times!

For 1971, the Daytona the changes were again limited – the new corporate handlebar switchgear, 'gargoyle' rear light shorter rear mudguard and indicators were standard fitments, and the headlamp was rubber mounted through the use of new 'ears' on the forks, but the frame, engine and running gear remained mostly unchanged. Noticeable was the use of the old-style front forks and brake – the Daytona did not

First and Last Daytona Specifications (and the pre-production T100D)

	1967 Daytona Super Sports (T100R)	1974 Daytona (T100R)	1974 (1/2) Daytona T100D
Engine			
Bore and stroke	69mm × 65.5mm	69mm × 65.5mm	69mm × 65.5mm
Capacity	490cc	490cc	490cc
Compression ratio	9:1	7.5:1	7.5:1
Power	41bhp at 7,200rpm	Not quoted	Not quoted
Carburettor			
Type	Amal Monobloc	Amal Concentric	Amal Concentric
Specification	376/324/5	R626/L626	R626/L626
Number	2	2	2
Transmission			
Engine sprocket (teeth)	26	26	26
Clutch sprocket (teeth)	58	58	58
Gearbox sprocket (teeth)	19	18	18
Rear sprocket (teeth)	46	47	47
RPM at 10mph (16km/h) in top gear	723	775	775
Gear ratios			
Top	5.4	5.82	5.82
Third	6.6	7.11	7.11
Second	8.66	9.38	9.38
First	13.38	14.39	14.39
Wheels and tyres			
Front	325 × 19	325 × 19	325 × 19
Rear	400 × 18	400 × 18	400 × 18
Front brake	8in (20cm) single leading shoe	8in (20cm) twin leading shoe	Hydraulic Triumph/Lockheed Disc
Rear brake	7in (18cm) single leading shoe	7in (18cm) single leading shoe	7in (18cm) single leading shoe
Dimensions			
Seat height	30in (76.2cm)	30in (76.2cm)	30in (76.2cm)
Wheelbase	53½in (136cm)	55in (139.7cm)	55in (139.7cm)
Length	83¼in (211.5cm)	84in (213.3cm)	84in (213.3cm)
Width	27in (68½cm)	29in (73.6cm)	29in (73.6cm)
Ground clearance	7⅛in (18.1cm)	7½in (19cm)	7½in (19cm)
Weight	340lb (154kg)	378lb (171kg)	378lb (171kg)
Fuel capacity	2⅞ US gal (10.8ltr)	3 UK gal (13.6ltr)	3 UK gal (13.6ltr)
Oil capacity	6 pints (3.4ltr)	5.8 pints (3.3ltr)	5.8 pints (3.3ltr)

A montage of Triumph shots of the 1970 Daytona in the UK.

adopt the alloy slider forks and conical hubs introduced on the rest of the range in 1971.

The colours were Olympic Flame and white. Moving into 1972, the dire situation at BSA Triumph meant that there were even fewer developments to the Daytona. Push in exhaust pipes, and a Cherry Red and Cold White fuel tank and mudguards were the main changes.

The situation remained largely unchanged for 1973, but with chrome-plated mudguards, rear grab rail, and Ice White flutes over Vermillion (bright red) on the tank.

For 1974, the fuel tank colour changed to Ice White flutes over Argosy Blue, and the silencers were changed to torpedo-shaped units to cope with increasingly stringent noise legislation. This was to be the final production variant of the Daytona, with all production ending when the Meriden workers started their sit-in in September 1973. Some of the bikes which were trapped inside the factory were released in 1974 and would have been registered in the UK with 1974 or 1975 number plate suffixes.

On the road the 1972 Daytona exemplified the Triumph ideals of good handling and road holding.

*The 1970 'C' Series exported to the US comprised the Daytona and T100C
Trophy. Painted in a flower power metallic purple, they certainly looked the part.*

*The 1970 Daytona was a clean, sleek machine, with the unmistakable
Triumph line.*

The purple 1970s range was sold on both sides of the Atlantic. Here is a British T100SS and Daytona going fishing.

Was stagnation one of the factors in Triumph's downfall? The styling of the 1972 Daytona, while good, was little changed from 1967.

This shot of a 1972 Daytona shows the slim profile of the bike.

The TR5T Adventurer/Trophy Trail (1973–4)

With the absence of the T100C in 1972, Triumph had no 'dual purpose' bike. The solution was to put the T100C motor into a frame derived from that used by the 1971-onwards BSA and Triumph unit singles. This amalgam was the TR5T Trophy Trail, or Adventurer, and was introduced late in 1972 for the 1973 model year.

While the engine was broadly speaking in the same state of tune as the 1971 T100C, retaining a single Amal Concentric carburettor, it needed a number of modifications to the top end to allow the head to be removed with the engine in the frame. The frame and the running gear had nothing in common with the previous models. The frame had a long ancestry, as it was based on the BSA offroad competition frame from the late 1960s which housed the excellent unit singles.

Production versions of the frame had first appeared in 1971 model ranges for both BSA and Triumph carrying the 250cc and 500cc unit single engines.

The all-welded, tubular construction carried the engine oil in a large-diameter top tube that extended underneath the seat, and a large-diameter single down tube. Together the tubing gave an oil capacity of 4¾ pints (UK), and the oil filler was positioned just behind the steering head. The engine sat in a duplex cradle and the rear swinging arm pivoted on needle roller bearings. In order to make the removal of the head possible with the engine in situ, the rocker boxes and the cylinder head central studs had to me modified. The rear chain adjustment was achieved by moving the front pivot of the swinging arm forwards and backwards in slots in the frame, with 'snail cam' plates locating on pins on the frame. One cam was fixed to the end of the swinging arm

The TR5T Adventurer/Trophy Trail was a fine successor to the T100C. The BSA single-derived frame was excellent on- or offroad.

The 1973 Adventurer 500 (TR5T)

1. Chrome front fender mounted high for off-road riding.
2. Small teardrop headlamp, chrome finish—quickly removable.
3. Enduro-type speedometer, adjustable trip odometer to 1/10 mile.
4. Quick removable turn signals mounted on handlebars.
5. Steel ball-ended clutch and brake levers.

6. Enduro-type handlebars.
7. Small switch console incorporates thumb-operated high/low beam lever and turn lever.
8. 2½ gallon polished alloy tank.
9. ¾-length competition saddle.
10. Tucked-in rear turn signals—quickly removable.

11. Class A tail light to meet 1973 federal specifications—polished alloy mounting bracket.
12. Newly-styled rear fender finished in bright chrome.
13. 53-tooth rear sprocket, 6.57:1 overall gear ratio.
14. 4.00x18 Trials tire—polished alloy conical rear hub.
15. 500cc vertical twin engine—one carburetor. Four-speed gearbox incorporates special internal ratios for trail and enduro riding.

16. Skid plate for engine protection.
17. Dual downswept exhaust fits into cannister-type silencer under gearbox. Also fitted with USDA-approved spark arrester. Low exhaust noise of 84.5 dbA.
18. 6⅝" fork travel—polished hard-chrome finish on stanchions.
19. Lightweight 6" front brake—conical design—finished in polished alloy.
20. 3.00x21 Dunlop Trials front tire.

ABOVE: The Adventurer/Trophy Trail had lots of good points, which were expanded on in the brochure.
BELOW: The Adventurer's exhaust system was not as attractive or practical as the T100C's upswept design.

The handlebar layout of the Adventurer included Yamaha switchgear on the left-hand side, and indicators mounted out of harm's way on the handlebars.

spindle; the other was bolted onto the other end of the pivot, making it difficult to misalign to rear wheel. The wheel itself was bolted into eyes at the end of the swinging arm. While the frame looked almost identical to the BSA/Triumph single's version, the engine mounts were subtly different, so dropping a 'C' Series engine into a BSA single frame is not as straightforward as it might seem.

The mudguards were chrome steel, and the front one was mounted on the bottom yoke, reducing unsprung weight and giving a modern offroad look. The front wheel had a 21in steel rim, with a 6in-diameter (15cm) single leading shoe brake carried in an alloy conical hub. The rear wheel was the same as those used by the rest of the 1973 Triumph range, with an 18in steel rim, and 7in-diameter (18cm) single leading shoe brake in an alloy conical hub.

Instruments comprised a speedometer and rev counter and were supplied by Nippon Denso, with chromed outer cases with integral fixing brackets that were fixed to the top yoke. The headlamp was a 6in (15cm) chrome item, and carried the Lucas three-position 57SA toggle light switch and three warning lights – high beam (blue/green), oil pressure (red) and indicators (amber).

The rear light was the latest Lucas type L917 tail light; it was carried on the corporate polished alloy bracket bolted to the rear mudguard and supported by a separate frame loop which bolted onto the rear shock absorber top mountings. The bike had indicators, Lucas type, with the rear ones fixed to the mudguard support loop on chromed steel stems. The front indicators were mounted on the wide, braced handlebars, making them less vulnerable in offroad use than if they were mounted on the headlamp as with the rest of the range. Handlebar switchgear for dip and main beam, indicators and horn was concentrated on the left-hand bar, and utilized an alloy Yamaha item, with all evidence of the Japanese make removed! The ignition switch was located on the right-hand side panel. The ignition coils and condensers were positioned on a plate behind the gearbox. A Lucas 2MC capacitor was mounted on a vibration isolating spring to enable the bike to operate without a bat-

1973/4 Triumph TR5T Adventurer/Trophy Trail (TR5T) Specification

Engine

Bore and stroke	69mm × 65.5mm
Capacity (cc)	490cc
Compression ratio	7.5:1
Power	Not Specified

Carburettor

Type	Amal Concentric
Specification	R928
Number	1

Transmission

Engine sprocket (teeth)	26
Clutch sprocket (teeth)	58
Gearbox sprocket (teeth)	18
Rear sprocket (teeth)	53
RPM at 10mph (16km/h) in top gear	857

Gear ratios

Top	6.57
Third	8.01
Second	11.56
First	18.65

Wheels and tyres

Front	300 × 21
Rear	400 × 18
Front brake	6in/15.2 cm Single leading shoe
Rear brake	7in/18 cm Single leading shoe

Dimensions

Seat height	32in (81cm)
Wheelbase	54in (137cm)
Length	85in (215cm)
Width	32in (81cm)
Ground clearance	7½in (19cm)
Weight	322lb (146kg)
Fuel capacity	2 US gal (9ltr)
Oil capacity	4 pints (2.25ltr)

tery. The Zener diode, used to regulate the battery charging current, was mounted on the lower yoke of the front forks, which, being alloy, made an effective heat sink. The horn was carried under the nose of the fuel tank.

The front forks were the corporate items, with alloy sliders, internal springs and exposed stanchions, but used alloy yokes as seen on the T25SS.

The exhaust system moved away from the standard Triumph upswept twin pipe and silencer systems seen previously. Two chromed exhaust pipes were a push fit into the cylinder head, with the timing-side one being held in position by a spring that connected to the front engine mount. These chromed pipes swept down the front of the engine, and then were bolted into a chromed Y-shaped collector pipe. This collector pipe ran inside the crankcase 'bash' plate, and connected to a large, black painted pressed steel silencer that sat under the engine and gearbox, with a single silencer exiting on the timing side running parallel to and under the swinging arm. A spark arrestor was fitted into the end of the silencer. It was not a particularly attractive system, but was discreet and was quiet – an important consideration with the ever more rigorous noise legislation. The alloy 2gal (9ltr) fuel tank was rubber mounted on the frame top tube using the BSA method of a single bolt and rubber bush in a tunnel through the centre of the tank, and a short dual seat was bolted onto the rear frame upper loop – interestingly, the seat was shorter than that fitted to the BSA road models, but longer than the single seat fitted to the B50MX offroader.

For 1973 the tank was finished with a yellow flash on either side of the tank, with a black- and gold-lined 'Triumph' stick-on logo on each side. The black side panels carried gold 'Trophy Trail' transfers, the mudguards were chromed and the frame and fitting were black. The bike changed very little for 1974, with the tank panels being coloured red, and gold 'Adventurer' transfers replacing the 'Trophy Trail' of the previous year. By all accounts the TR5T was a successful compromise between road and trail, and was favourably received by the press at the time. It was successful in the 1973 ISDT, held in the US, and is now a sought-after model in its own right.

The End of the Line: the Prototype T100D Daytona 'Series 2' and the Meriden Blockade Bikes (1975–6)

The 'C' Series story did not quite finish with the Daytona and the Adventurer/Trophy Trail. As the British motorcycle industry entered its death throes, there was still some activity.

The last T100D was Triumph's last gasp for the 'C' Series twins. It shared the disc brakes front end with the 750cc twins, giving the bike a more up-to-date look and improved braking.

The final Daytona was the T100D – the Series 2. This model was developed during 1972–3 to use a greater proportion of standard parts from the corporate parts bin, taking much of the running gear from the oil in frame 'B' Series 750cc models, the T140 Bonneville, and TR7 Tiger. The main change was the use of the new style Ceriani-type forks and the fitting of a disc brake – essentially the whole front end was the same as the disc-braked 750cc T140 Bonneville that was introduced in 1973.

New silencers, the same as those fitted to the 750cc Bonneville and a conical rear hub made up the visible changes to the bike, while a number of engine improvements were also made. Altogether twelve pre-production bikes were made, and were in varying stages of completion when the Meriden sit-in began. A number survive today as a glimpse of what might have been.

The very last new 'C' Series twins came onto the UK market in 1976, when the Meriden sit in was in full flow, and the workers at the plant 'released' some bikes to Norton Villiers Triumph. NVT in turn distributed these bikes to their UK dealers, and among them were a batch of 1974-specification Daytonas. These bikes had been languishing in the factory for a year or so, but were sold reasonably quickly. The provided much needed cash flow for NVT, but many had suffered during their enforced inactivity, and the customers found numerous problems with the bikes. See Simon Smith's experiences later on in this book!

The T100D silencers were also shared with the T140, and met the conditions of the latest noise legislation.

The Last Twin – The Triumph Bandit and BSA Fury

Edward Turner's final design for the British bike industry was a replacement for the 'C' Series twins. Turner took on the job after he had retired from BSA-Triumph and presented the prototype bike to Triumph in 1968. The bike was a 350cc twin, with gear-driven double overhead cams (dohc) and had a single down tube frame that was pretty flimsy and appeared to be derived from the Tiger Cub.

The engine followed a practice used by the Japanese (notably Honda) on their smaller four-stroke twins in that it used a 180-degree crank-shaft, where when one piston was at top dead centre, the other was at bottom dead centre. While this configuration gave uneven firing impulses, it had better primary balance than the traditional British 360-degree twin, where the pistons rise and fall in parallel. One interesting point with the engine was that although it conformed to the typical British layout, with the clutch sitting on a countershaft in front of the final drive sprocket, the whole engine was a mirror image of the bikes made to date, with the timing side on the left, and the primary and final drive on the right. This was to ensure the gear change lever was set on the left-hand side to comply with American legislation that was looming, but without having to design a completely different 'crossover'-type gearbox.

The running gear was conventional, apart from the provision of a cable-operated front disc brake, a forward-thinking design feature that was way ahead of the then current thinking on brakes. Bert Hopwood, Triumph's chief engineer at the time and author of Whatever Happened to the British Motorcycle Industry (see bibliography) had the unenviable task of assessing Turner's prototype and getting it into production. In his book he describes what happened. While the performance of the bike was good, when Hopwood started testing, a number of problems were exposed. In a report to the board, he stated that the test bench engine had been run for the equivalent of 1,500 road miles (2,400km) and there had been two crankshaft breakages and one

The Turner-designed engine was flimsy and failed regularly during testing. However, it gives a lot of power for its size.

failure of the valve train. The actual road test bike had had to have the frame completely redesigned, and the forks replaced to make it suitable for road use.

This bike was using 4 pints of oil every 100 miles, and had suffered from crankshaft, main bearing, and gudgeon pin failures. The frame was considered to be too flimsy, and the front forks were flimsy enough to be considered dangerous. So the prototype had to be completely reworked to make a decent bike. In the final bikes, the engine was still a 350cc double overhead cam 120-degree twin, but, as Bert Hopwood wrote in Whatever Happened to the British Motorcycle Industry, just about the only thing not changed in the engine was the valve angle, and the rolling chassis was completely new.

The engine was of unit construction, with the cylinders slanted forwards by 15 degrees, and although maintaining the traditional gearbox configuration of concentric clutch and main shafts, the engine layout was a mirror image of previous Triumph twins, with the primary and final drives on its right-hand side. Bore and stroke were 63mm × 56mm, giving a capacity of just

over 349cc, and the very 'over square' short stroke engine was good for higher revs. The timing chain drive and BSA-type double gear oil pump were located on the left-hand side of the engine. The crankshaft was of relatively conventional design, with oil fed through the end of the crank to the big ends, and the main bearings were the usual ball on the timing side and heavier-duty roller on the drive side.

The main difference to other Triumph twin cranks was the use of 180-degree spacing of the crankpins. Triumph publicity at the time stated this was to reduce vibration at high revs, which it does, but the configuration introduces a different sort of vibration inducing effect known as 'rocking couple'. To avoid or minimize the rocking couple vibration, the crank's width and the distance between the pistons needs to be kept as short as possible. The downside of this was that there was very little space between the cylinders, which would have made it difficult to simply bore the engine out to make a 500cc twin. Increasing the stroke of the engine would have resulted in a very long stroke of some

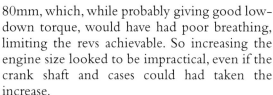

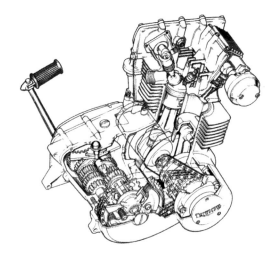

ABOVE: *The cutaway of the Bandit engine shows the DOHC head, electric start and other details.*

LEFT: *The redesigned engine retained Turner's layout and the double overhead cams. It was a lot more reliable than the original Turner designed motor, though, and almost made it into production.*

80mm, which, while probably giving good low-down torque, would have had poor breathing, limiting the revs achievable. So increasing the engine size looked to be impractical, even if the crank shaft and cases could had taken the increase.

The one-piece alloy barrel had iron liners, and the alloy flat-topped pistons gave a compression ratio of 9.5:1. The double overhead cams were driven from the timing side by a long single chain. The inverted L-shaped cam chain drive case was a distinctive feature of the engine, with a blade-type chain tensioner carried inside the case. The contact breaker points and mechanical advance/retard unit were carried under a round cover on the end of the exhaust cam on the drive side. The two valves per cylinder were operated directly from the cams using buckets, with adjustment being carried out using shims. Carburetion was provided by twin 26mm Amal Concentric instruments, which were mounted on separate manifolds that were mounted via rubber tubes to the screw in inlet pots in the head.

The primary drive was conventional, with a multi-plate four-spring clutch being driven from the crank through a duplex chain. Provision for an electric starter was made, with a Lucas starter motor being mounted on top of the crankcases behind the cylinders, and connected to the crank shaft by a single row chain that drove a third row of teeth on the engine drive sprocket. The 110w Lucas alternator also lived in the primary chain case, with its rotor bolted to the crankcases and its stator driven directly on the end of the crank shaft.

The gearbox was similar in layout to the 'C' Series twins but had a number of differences. These included five speeds, a kick starter quadrant like that used on the 'B' Series twins, and a circular gear selector cam plate.

The bike that finally made it almost into production bore little or no resemblance to Turner's prototype, and was badged either as the Triumph Bandit or the BSA Fury. Differences between the BSA and Triumph variants seem to have been limited to paint and badges. The Triumph bikes came in two variants – the T35SS (Street Scrambler) and the T35R (Road). The frame was all new, with no resemblance to Turner's Cub-derived trellis, and seems to have been a derivative of a racing frame made by Rod North for one of Percy Tait's racers. The frame was a double cradle, all-welded lightweight affair, which weighed just 23lb (10.5kg). The twin front tubes swept down from the headstock, under the engine, then back to brace the top rear shock absorber mount and support the top seat loop, forming a wide U shape. A second pair of tubes was welded to this U just above the rear of the engine; they were angled forwards, running just behind the engine to join up with the rest of the frame at the headstock. A tubular swinging arm was securely located between the main cradle. The frame was generally considered to excellent, being very rigid and giving superb handling and road holding.

The rest of the running gear was sourced from the Umberslade Hall-designed components used on the rest of the range for the 1971 model year.

The Ceriani style front forks carried the new corporate 8in (20cm) diameter twin leading shoe brake in an alloy conical hub, while the rear conical hub had the 7in (18cm) single leading shoe brake. The 'standard' rear wheel had to be turned around so that the final drive sprocket was on the right hand side – the opposite side to the rest of the range. Both wheels were 18in (45cm) in diameter and tyres were Dunlop K70s 325 × 18 on the front, and 350 × 18 on the rear. The fuel tank was slim in profile, but wide enough to have a capacity of 2¾ US gallons. The fuel tank was painted in a pale green – called Jealous Green by Triumph – and on each side of the tank there were two black flashes, above and below the Triumph logo, which were lined in white. The T35SS had chromed mudguards, while the T35R's were painted Jealous Green. The frame was finished in black enamel, thus escaping the infamous Dove Grey finish applied to the BSA derivatives, and side panels were finished in Silver with a black lower section. The electrical system was the standard Lucas 12v

The Triumph Bandit was designated T35. It appeared as a Road model (T35R) when equipped with low pipes, as pictured here in the 1971 Triumph brochure.

ABOVE: *The Street Scrambler (T35SS) model had a high-level exhaust on the drive (left-hand) side.*

OPPOSITE: *There are some Bandits in captivity – this is the T35R model in the Sammy Millar museum in New Milton, Hampshire, in the UK. The 1971 Triumph/BSA corporate wheels and forks are visible.*

LEFT: *Another shot of the Sammy Millar museum T35R. The contact breaker point's cover is the exhaust camshaft and the electric starter is visible behind the cylinder barrels.*

set-up as seen across the range, with the new corporate switchgear on the handlebars and flashing direction indicators as standard.

The Road model (T35R) came with a chrome low-level exhaust system, with a balance pipe between the two sides running under the rear of the engine cradle and a megaphone-type silencer on both sides. The Street Scrambler (T35SS) had a high-level system running on the right-hand side, with the black-finished exhaust pipes running over the top of the primary chain case, and connecting into a black exhaust box which was styled to resemble two megaphone silencers but was in fact a single unit – hence there was no balance pipe between the exhaust pipes.

While the bike made it into the 1971 brochure, the problems encountered with rushing it into production, combined with the dubious state of the BSA-Triumph group's finances, meant that the plug was pulled on the project just as the experimental department had completed the first batch of approximately eighteen pre-production bikes and were starting to set up the production line proper. The pre-production bikes were displayed at various shows around the world and shown to dealers in the USA and Australia during 1970. A production schedule dated 5 November 1970 shows the proposed delivery date of the Bandit T35SS to be March 1971, followed by the T35R in April.

Sadly no production bikes were produced. However, a large number of frames had been brought in and a number of these have reappeared housing 'B' Series and 'C' Series Triumph engines, and even BSA A65 units.

An intriguing postscript to the above can be found in Peter Hartley's book *The Ariel Story* (see bibliography). In the book, he reveals that while the Bandit/Fury was being developed, a prototype was built using the Bandit engine in an Ariel frame. Called the Ariel Impala, and presented as the last Ariel, details are scarce. However, what is certain is that it never made it into production.

3 Technical Description and Development

The Triumph 'C' range twins represented a major step forward for the Triumph marque, giving the company a third distinctive range of machines, the others being the pre-unit 500 and 650cc machines (the 'B' Range) and the diminutive 200cc Tiger Cub (the 'A' Range).

The new range also set Triumph apart from the competition, in having a 500cc twin derived from a 350cc machine, making the 500cc models light and wieldy in comparison to the other British 500cc twins such as the BSA A50. When Edward Turner visited Japan in 1960, he relates how the chief of operations at Honda, Benjiro Honda, had some firm opinions about the British motor cycle industry:

Mr Honda expressed great respect and admiration for the British Motorcycle Industry, and said that, though some of our products were old fashioned, he was not deceived by this as he thought the 'C' range of Triumph (350cc/500cc) was equally up to date in comparison with anything being made in Japan.

So were the Japanese being polite to Turner? Even at that time their engineering skills and investment in modern machine tools was resulting in brand new designs, while the Triumph range gave more than a nod to its past.

This chapter explores the design of the range, starting with the introduction of the 350cc Twenty-one, and describes each

The 1958 Twenty-one was innovative with its enclosure, but the styling was not to everyone's taste.

The final development of the Twenty-one was the Daytona. Here is a 1970 UK model, with the traditional Triumph styling.

of the main components (engine, gearbox, frame, and so on) of the initial model, and the changes made to the components as the range evolved. As before, the timing side is the right-hand side of the bike, and the drive side the left, with the rider sitting on the bike.

The following sections describe each part of the Twenty-one as it was on its introduction, then summarizes the major changes made to the various parts through the life of the 'C' series twins.

Engine, Primary Drive and Gearbox

The Triumph Twenty-one was not Edward Turner's first unit construction engine – that honour went to the 150cc Terrier and 200cc Tiger Cub – but it was Turner and Triumph's first unit construction twin.

The Twenty-one engine unit was a four stroke vertical twin, with its pistons rising and falling together. Each cylinder was set up to fire when the other was on its exhaust stroke, giving a 360-degree firing interval – one bang per revolution. The engine's bore and stroke was 58.25mm by 65.5mm, giving a capacity of 348cc. The unit was softly tuned, and had a claimed power output was a modest 18.5bhp at 6,500rpm, and a compres-

sion ratio of 7.5:1. The Twenty-one's crankcase was constructed from two alloy castings that contained the crankshaft assembly, the gearbox and primary drive.

The crankcases were split vertically to contain the crankshaft, and the drive side casing incorporated the inner primary chain case extending behind the crank. The timing side crankcase incorporated the gearbox housing behind the crank, which extended across the centreline towards the primary chain case. The engine, primary chain case and the gearbox were all separate from each other and had separate independent oil supplies. Four further casings were used in the bottom end to finish off the engine cases: a smoothly styled primary chain case, a traditionally styled rounded triangular timing case, and inner and outer gearbox covers.

The engine configuration followed the layout pioneered by the Speed Twin, with twin camshafts fore and aft of the crankshaft. The camshafts were supported by phosphor bronze bushes in the drive-side crankcase, but had large-diameter bearings on the timing side that ran directly in the aluminium crankcase with no bushes. On the timing side, the camshafts were

The 3TA engine unit was a compact and clean design. Note the distributor tucked behind the barrels, with its extensive rubber boot to help waterproofing.

Machining the crankcases for the 'C' Series twins.

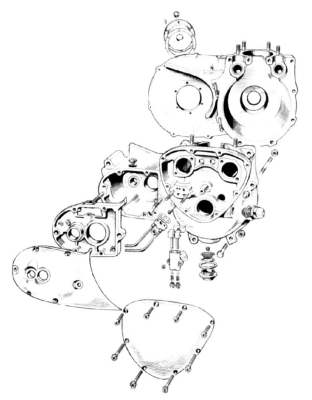

The unit construction crankcases were sturdy and stiff, and changed only in detail throughout the model's life.

ABOVE: Machining the crank in the factory was done with automated tools.

RIGHT: The one-piece crank had a bolt-on flywheel, and camshafts were driven by a gear train on the timing side in the traditional Triumph layout.

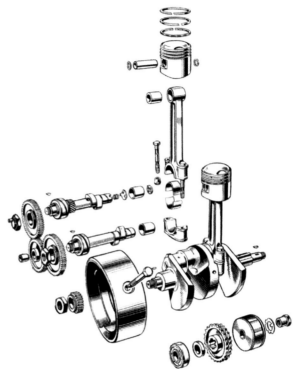

located by diamond-shaped steel retaining plates, which were bolted onto the outside face of the crankcase and could be removed without splitting the cases. Each camshaft had a gear keyed to it, which engaged with a central intermediate gear which was driven from a pinion on the end of the crank.

In a classic Turner touch, the inlet camshaft also carried a worm drive in its centre that was used to drive the ignition distributor, had a timed rotary breather valve in its drive-side end, and was fitted with an eccentric peg on its pinion-retaining bolt to drive the plunger-type oil pump. Hence there was no need for any auxiliary drives to complicate the engine design and sap power. The timing gears and oil pump were covered by the trademark triangular timing cover, with the traditional triangular patent plate in its centre giving a family look to the new engine. The ignition distributor sat behind the cylinder barrels.

Lubrication System

The crank shaft followed established Triumph practice, and was a single forging in EN16B steel, with a separate central flywheel bolted to a central web with three radial bolts. The crank pins were positioned each side of the central web, and were set to give a 360-degree crank throw. Outboard of the crank pins were two bob weights which carried the main shafts. The big ends used plain bearings, steel-backed micro Babbitt shells produced by Vandervell, and the connecting rods were steel stampings rather than Triumph's traditional light alloy 'Hiduminiun'. The small ends comprised wrapped Vandervell bushes. The crankshaft ran on two main bearings, the drive side being a ball journal and the timing side a plain bearing lined with Vandervell VP3 copper lead alloy. The timing side end of the crank carried a single timing pinion, with its position fixed by a woodruff key and secured with a right-

RIGHT: Triumph started the 'C' Series range using steel con rods in the 3TA. The range eventually moved to alloy con rods.

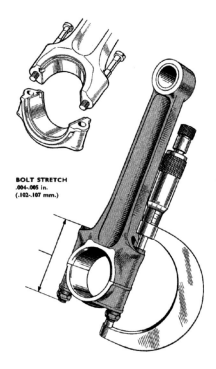

BOLT STRETCH
.004-.005 in.
(.102-.107 mm.)

BELOW: Triumph's plunger oil pump is a simple and reliable design, which does the job. With its built-in ball valves, wet sumping is rarely a problem.

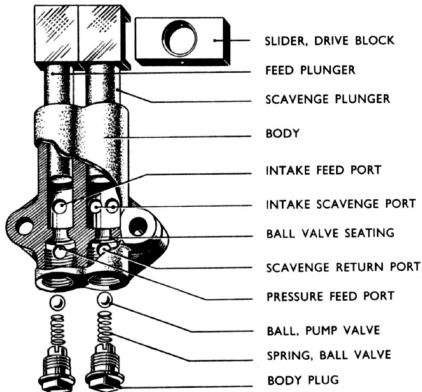

SLIDER, DRIVE BLOCK

FEED PLUNGER

SCAVENGE PLUNGER

BODY

INTAKE FEED PORT

INTAKE SCAVENGE PORT

BALL VALVE SEATING

SCAVENGE RETURN PORT

PRESSURE FEED PORT

BALL, PUMP VALVE

SPRING, BALL VALVE

BODY PLUG

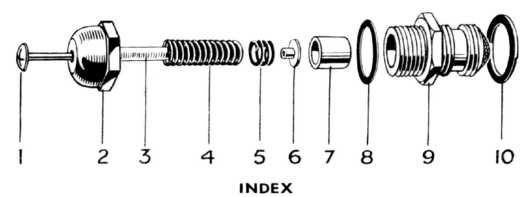

INDEX

I	Indicator Shaft	5	Auxiliary Spring	8	Cap Washer
2	Valve Cap	6	Shaft Nut	9	Body
3	Rubber Seal	7	Piston	10	Body Washer
4	Main Spring				

ABOVE: Oil pressure is limited on the Triumph engine by this simple valve – excess pressure is dumped into the sump.

BELOW: The 3TA lubrication system was simple and effective. Oil fed into the crank via the main bearing bush lubricated the big ends.

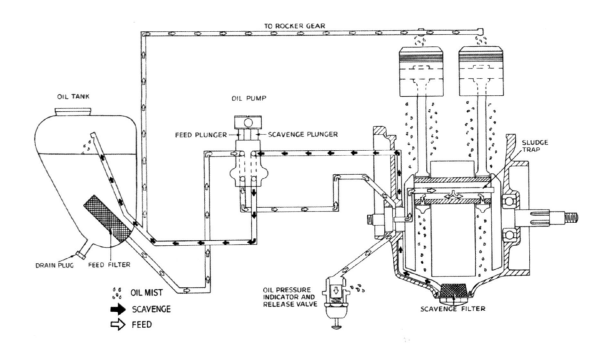

hand-threaded nut. The drive side of the crank shaft was splined along approximately half its length to carry the primary drive engine sprocket, and then had a parallel length to carry the alternator rotor, which was positioned with a woodruff key and fixed in place with a nut.

The engine used the traditional Triumph dry sump lubrication system, where the oil was stored in a separate tank rather than in the engine sump. Oil was pumped under pressure into the engine (fed), then fell into a small sump at the lowest point of the engine and was then pumped back (or scavenged) back into the oil tank. To achieve these two actions – the feed and scavenge – the oil pump needs to have sides. The feed side pumps the oil into the engine, and the scavenge side pumps the oil from the sump back to the oil tank. The scavenge side of the pump had twice the capacity of the feed side, ensuring that the sump would not fill with oil while the engine was running. The pump was driven from an eccentric pin on the inlet camshaft securing nut using a sliding block. The Twenty-one used the traditional Triumph twin plunger design for its oil pump, a well-proved design used on the Speed Twin.

The two plungers were of different diameter to ensure the scavenge side could pass more oil than was being pumped into the engine, and was controlled by ball and spring non-return valves to ensure the oil was pumped in the right direction. One major advantage of this type of pump over gear-type pumps as used by BSA and Norton twins is that they are not prone to wet sumping. This phenomenon, whereby oil leaks from the tank through the pump into the engine's sump if the engine is not run for a while, is largely prevented by the close fit of the plungers in the pump body – wet sumping in a Triumph is usually indicative of a very badly worn pump and a sticking non-return valve.

Once the oil had been pumped from the oil tank through the feed side of the pump, it was fed via drillings in the crankcases into the timing side main bearing bush. A separate drilling led to a pressure-relief valve, placed on the front of the timing case, which would blow off any excess oil

pressure by diverting oil back to the sump. The valve comprised a spring-loaded plunger in a domed nut, which incorporated the famous Triumph button indicator, which would stick out when there was pressure present. Oil fed through the bush was directed through drillings to a gallery through the crank pins that fed the big end bearings, and then fell into the sump, lubricating the pistons and drive side main bearing by splash. Triumph claimed the oil issued from the big ends in the form of a fog to lubricate the pistons and other engine parts, and the system worked well. Oil in the sump was scavenged back to the oil pump via a pickup in the sump. A feed to rocker gear in the cylinder head was taken off the return feed.

Oil filtration was by wire mesh filters in the oil tank feed and the engine sump, while a sludge trap was used in the crank. The sludge trap was a tube in the gallery in the crankshaft that led to the big end bearing. Oil was fed into the tube, and then escaped into the gallery and hence the big ends through drillings in the tube. Particles suspended in the oil would be centrifuged out in the tube, and form a sludge in the tube rather than damage the big end bearings.

The lubrication system was well thought out and based on sound principles, and gave very few problems in service. The only problem area was the oil feed to the crank through the timing-side main bush. If the bush became excessively worn, this could result in a lowering of oil pressure to the big ends. Eventually, if an owner ignored the rumbling from the bottom end, the drive-side big end (the one furthest from the oil feed) would fail. However, anecdotal evidence for such a failure is, in my experience, rare and certainly less common than the failure of the similar system used on the BSA A50/A65.

Cylinder Block and Head

Moving up the engine, the one-piece cylinder block was cast iron and heavily finned, with the fins extending onto the base flange, and was finished in silver paint to give the appearance of an all-alloy motor.

The cylinder barrel was cast iron but was painted silver to give the illusion of alloy.

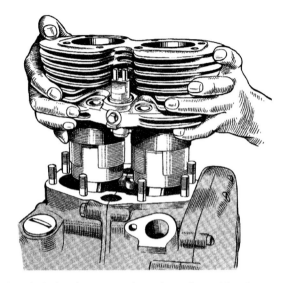

The cylinder barrel was spigotted into the crankcases. Note the distributor drive hole behind the barrels.

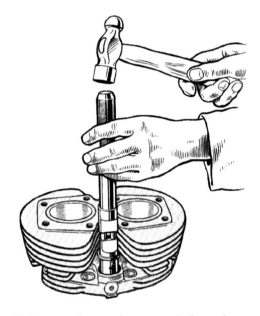

Separate blocks were used to carry the tappets at the front and rear of the barrels, rather than carrying the tappets directly in the barrel.

The block was tunnelled centrally to provide decent cooling, and was fixed to the crankcases using eight studs.

Front and back, above the camshafts, were the tappet blocks which each carried two tappets (cam followers), and were a press fit in the cylinder block front and rear. The tappets operated light alloy pushrods that were encased in chromed tubes front and rear.

The tops of the push rod tubes located in the cylinder head, and while their bottom joints were sealed with rubber washers and the top with heat-resistant silicone rubber seals, they were prone to oil leakage throughout the life of the model. The oil fed to the top end drained down to the sump via the pushrod tubes. Pistons were die cast in 'LO-EX' (low expansion) aluminium alloy, and were fitted with three rings – a plain-faced compression ring in the top groove, a tapered middle ring and an oil scraper ring in the bottom groove. The gudgeon pins were made of nickel chrome steel, and were retained in the piston by circlips. The pistons were slightly domed with cutaways for the valves, and in the Twenty-one had a compression ratio of 7.5:1.

The cylinder head was cast in DTD424 light aluminium alloy. The valve seats were of austenitic iron and the combustion chambers were hemispherical. The valve angle was 80 degrees and the inlet valves were 1¾in in diameter, and the exhaust valves 1⅜in. The inlet valves were made from silichrome steel, while the more heavily stressed exhaust valves were made from Jessop G2 steel. Exhaust ports had screw-in steel adaptors which the exhaust pipes clamped to. Bolted to the cylinder head were two light alloy rocker boxes that carried the rockers and associated tappets on spindles. The rocker oil feed was fed into the rocker boxes through the top of the casting, rather than through the rocker spindles as was normal on the pre-unit Triumphs. Tappet adjustment was made through round tappet covers.

Primary Drive and Clutch

The primary drive was encased by a polished alloy chain case, fixed to the inner chain case on the drive side crankcase with 10 Philips screws. The engine sprocket fitted on the splined engine main shaft, and drove a pre-stretched duplex primary chain, which transmitted power to the clutch outer basket.

The clutch's four springs were mounted on a pressure plate, which bore on the four friction drive and five plain drive plates, and the clutch centre incorporated a rubber vane-type shock absorber. The clutch was mounted on the gearbox main shaft, and was operated by a pushrod that passed through the hollow main shaft and lifted the pressure plate against the four springs. Clutch adjustment was carried out using an adjuster pin that screwed into the pressure plate and bore on the push rod. Access to the adjuster was through a screw-in slotted plug on the face of the outer chain case. The duplex primary chain was claimed by Triumph to be a special pre-stretched type, which did not require a tensioner. Also residing in the primary chain case was the RM13/15 alternator, with its stator mounted on three studs on the inner chain case, and the rotor mounted on the end of the crank. The primary chain case oil was filled via a slotted cap on the top of the inner chain case part of the drive-side crankcase.

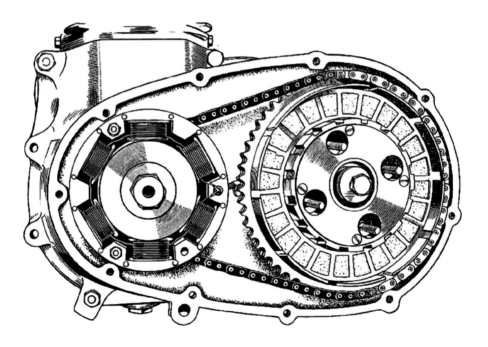

The primary drive used a duplex chain, with a tensioner only appearing later in the model's life. Note the early alternator, with its bare coils exposed to the hostile environment of the chain case.

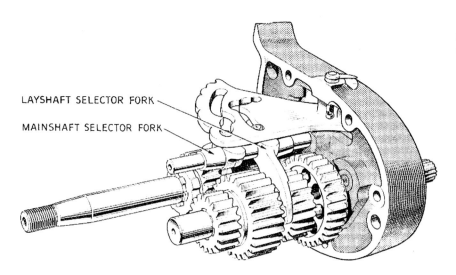

The gear cluster is compact. The gear indicator on the top of the case is fixed to the selector quadrant axis.

LAYSHAFT SELECTOR FORK

MAINSHAFT SELECTOR FORK

Gearbox

The gearbox was a four-speed unit with the lay shaft located behind the main shaft. The box was obviously based on the Terrier/Tiger Cub model, but was substantially beefed up and proved to be reliable in service. The gearbox followed standard Triumph practice, with power being fed into the main shaft via the clutch, being transmitted through the gearbox and exiting to the rear chair sprockets via a sleeve gear that was concentric to the main shaft. The gearbox sprocket was located behind the clutch, outside the chain case. Gear selection was controlled by a cam plate, mounted horizontally above the gear cluster, which pivoted on a vertical pin that also operated the gear indicator on the top of the gearbox. A gearbox inner cover carried the timing side gearbox bearings, along with the selector cam plate and the kick starter mechanism, while the gearbox outer case carried the gear selector mechanism and the clutch operating mechanism. The gear lever was fixed to a splined shaft on the outside of the casing, and, unusually the kick starter lever was also splined onto its shaft – most other Triumphs and BSAs made do with a cotter pin to fix their kick starter levers.

The kick start lever is splined to its shaft – unlike the larger or smaller models in the Triumph range, which used a cheaper cotter pin fixing.

While not breaking any new ground, the 350cc unit engine was considered to be up to date at the time, and remained largely unchanged throughout the life of the 'C' Series models. Producing a claimed 18.5 horsepower, the unit was understressed and capable of substantial development.

Engine Development

The development of the original unit went in two directions – tune up the 350 and raise the capacity to 500cc – as the Americans said, there's no substitute for cubes! Tuning the 350cc unit gave rise to the Tiger 90, which was the only development of the 350cc unit, and produced 27bhp. This was almost as much power as the first 500cc units. Increasing the capacity of the 350cc unit to 500cc gave an immediate power boost, with the first Speed Twin giving 27bhp, and the 1971 T100R/T100D Daytona producing a claimed 41bhp.

The Tiger 90, introduced for 1963, gained its power boost through 'standard' tuning methods. While the bore and stroke remained the same as on the 3TA unit, the compression ratio was raised to 9:1. The T90 also lost the distrib-

utor, with twin Lucas 4CA contact breaker points housed under a neat cover in the timing case and were driven from the end of the exhaust camshaft. A mechanical advance retard mechanism was housed behind the timing cover, and employed bob weights and springs to control the movement of the timing cam. The T90 was finally discontinued at the end of the 1968 model year.

The 500cc unit engine was first introduced in the 5TA Speed Twin in 1959. Essentially the unit was an overbored 3TA, with bore and stroke of 69mm × 65.5mm, but was broadly in the same state of tune as the 3TA. The 5TA engine had a compression ration of 7:1, which was lower than that of the 3TA, and gave a claimed 27bhp at 6,500rpm. It was fitted with a larger Amal Monobloc 375/35 carburettor. The unit was progressively and successfully developed to reliably provide more power. The performance-oriented development of the 500cc unit started with the 1960 T100A, which featured a higher compression ratio of 9:1 and E3325 cams. These modifications enabled the engine to rev higher despite it having the same carburettor as the 5TA, and upped the engine power to 32bhp at 7,000rpm.

The Daytona engine had points inside rather than the distributor and twin carburettors – but otherwise was very similar to the original 3TA.

ABOVE: The 5TA engine was a handsome unit, which contributed to the range's modern looks.

BELOW: The later models boasted a primary chain tensioner, accessed from the outer chain case.

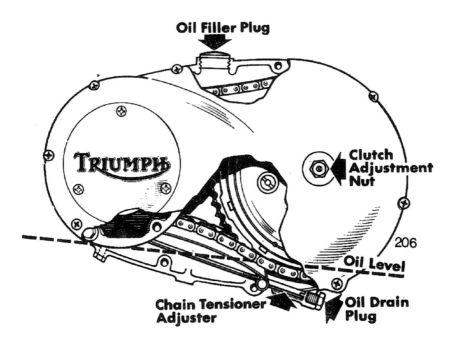

The only downside of the T100A was its energy transfer ignition, which meant either difficult starting or poor high-speed running, and was soon dropped for road use. Development continued, however, and for 1961 a larger carburettor (376/273) was specified, and E3134 type cams installed, increasing power to 34bhp. The 500cc unit also gained a much-needed primary chain tensioner in 1960, which was also fitted to the 3TA. This was the traditional Triumph sprung blade type, with its front located on a dowel in the inner chain case, and the screw adjustor located in the chain case outer cover – making it awkward to remove the outer cover.

The T100A unit was replaced in 1962 with the T100SS, which had the E3325 exhaust camshaft but still produced 34bhp. For 1964, the 500cc unit gained twin contact breaker points in the timing cover while losing the distributor, and a new design of cylinder head was fitted; in this form the T100 unit was continued into 1965 and 1966. The 5TA unit was quietly dropped at the end of the 1966 season. The experiences of the works ride in Daytona in 1966 saw a raft of improvements to the engines with the introduction of the T100T Daytona.

The main external difference between the T100T and the T100SS was the twin Amal Monobloc carburettors fitted to the T100T, which enabled the engine to give 39bhp at 7,400rpm. Along with the twin carbs came a new head, with the valve set at 39 degrees rather than the previous model's 45 degrees, and with the Daytona having larger inlet valves (1$\frac{17}{32}$in as opposed to the T100SS at 1$\frac{3}{16}$in). The T100T reverted to E3134 cams for inlet and exhaust, and the exhaust cam was fitted with a rev counter drive slot on the left-hand side. Detail improvements were made for 1968, with the T100S getting the Daytona head, and the new Amal 626 Concentrics replacing the Amal Monobloc carburettor.

Probably the most significant change to the 500cc unit engine was made in 1969, with the introduction of a new ball bearing for the timing-side main bearing, replacing the bush that had served the unit well but which was beginning to wilt under the pressure of the ever-increasing demands for more power.

With the introduction of the new timing-side main bearing, the drive side main bearing was up-rated to a roller type. The oil feed to the

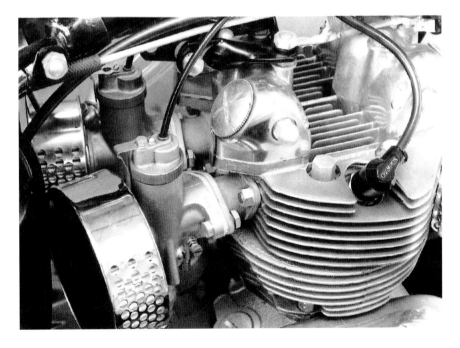

The first Daytona of 1967 was equipped with twin Amal Monobloc carburettors.

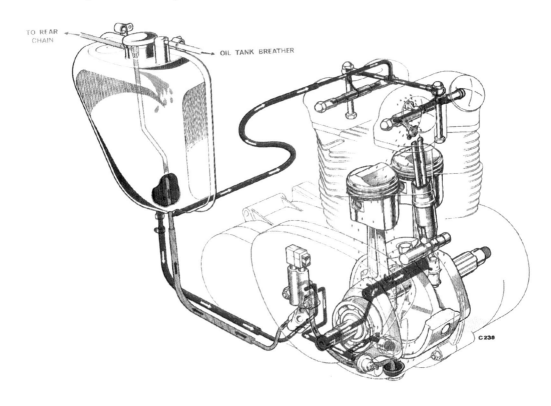

ABOVE: *The change over to a timing-side main ball bearing in 1969 meant modifications were necessary to the oil feed to the crank. The feed was taken through the end of the crank.*

LEFT: *The new main bearings for 1969 meant modifications to the timing cover to take the new oil end feed to the crank. Two new bulges are visible, along with a new oil pressure switch.*

big ends was now fed into the end of the crank through new oil ways in the timing cover, giving a much more consistent feed. The new bearing also enabled the crank to be positively located by clamping it onto the new timing-side main. This modification also included an oil pressure warning light switch in the front of the timing case.

Up top, the head was modified to accommodate castellated push rod tubs, which improved the chances of getting an oil-tight seal. The rocker boxes were also modified with a small screw plug in their outside edges to ease the task of tappet adjustment – the holes were big enough to get the feeler gauge in to set the gap.

The same year also saw the move towards standardizing on the American UNF/UNC thread forms, although only some components were converted.

The final major change to engine occurred in 1970, with the introduction of a new breathing system. Up until then, the engine breathed through a timed valve driven off the end of the inlet camshaft. While this worked, it was not ideal and was replaced by a much simpler system. The drive-side oil seal on the crank was removed, so the engine could 'breathe' into the primary chain case. A large-diameter pipe was run from the top of the chain case to vent the pressure. Finally three small holes were drilled in the wall of the chain case to allow any excess oil that collected in the chain case to be drained back into the crankcase, where it could be scavenged from the sump back to the oil tank. It was a simple, effective system that probably did more to help keep the engine oil tight than any other modification.

The engine was in production in this form to the end of the line. The only other major changes that were made to unit concerned the TR5T unit, which had the inner head bolts and rocker box fixings modified to allow the head and rocker boxes to be fitted and removed with the engine in the frame. The modifications were needed because of the wide oil-carrying top tube used in the BSA unit single-derived frame.

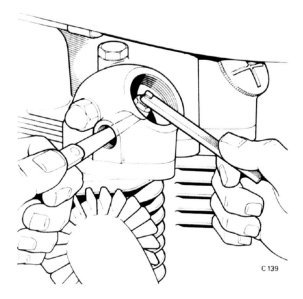

The final 'C' Series bikes had an extra access hole in the rocker covers to improve access to adjust the valve clearances.

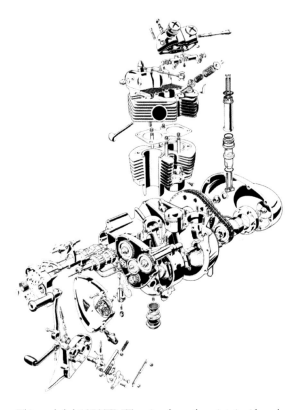

This exploded 1973 TR5T engine shows the points in side and end feed crank of the final version of the 'C' Series engine.

Carburation

There were two main types of carburettor used on the 'C' Series twins, both made by Amal. The range started off using the Monobloc, and switched to the Concentric in 1968.

The Amal Monobloc was innovative when it first appeared in the 1950s as it had its float bowl incorporated into the main casting – hence the name. This meant that there were no leak-prone joints between the float chamber and the main carburettor, and it also meant that the float height was fixed, removing a problem area for amateur engine tuners!

One slight problem with the Monobloc was that the adjustment screws (pilot jet and throttle stop) were on the opposite side to the float bowl cover. While this was not a problem with a single carburettor set-up, with twin carburettors it meant either the adjusters or the float bowl would be difficult to access. This problem was alleviated to a certain point by making 'handed' carburettor bodies – however, this was an expensive way to go, as it meant a completely different casting for the each side.

The Monobloc built itself a good reputation, being easy to set up and tune, and reliable in service. The side mounting of the float bowl cover,

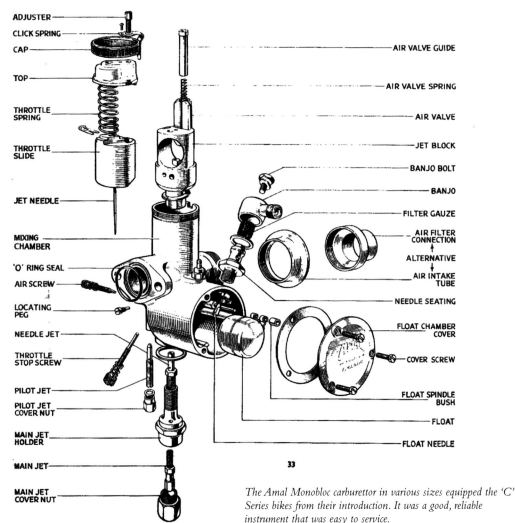

33

The Amal Monobloc carburettor in various sizes equipped the 'C' Series bikes from their introduction. It was a good, reliable instrument that was easy to service.

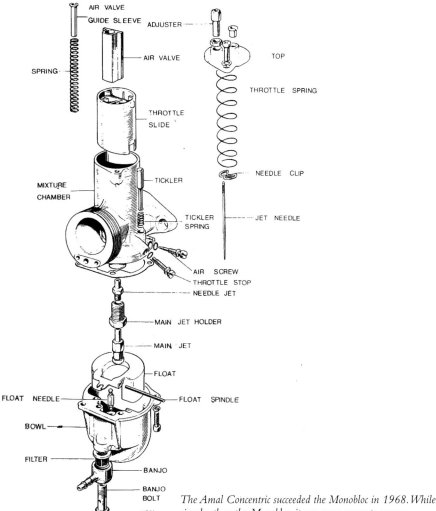

AIR VALVE

GUIDE SLEEVE   ADJUSTER

AIR VALVE

TOP

SPRING

THROTTLE SPRING

THROTTLE
SLIDE

MIXTURE
CHAMBER

TICKLER

NEEDLE CLIP

TICKLER
SPRING

JET NEEDLE

AIR SCREW

THROTTLE STOP

NEEDLE JET

MAIN JET HOLDER

MAIN JET

FLOAT

FLOAT NEEDLE

FLOAT SPINDLE

BOWL

FILTER

BANJO

BANJO
BOLT

B261

*The Amal Concentric succeeded the Monobloc in 1968. While
simpler than the Monobloc, it was more prone to wear.*

and the bottom-mounted main jet cover nut, meant that any debris or water in the carburettor could be quickly sorted out at the roadside. However, Amal were under pressure from BSA and Triumph to produce a cheaper instrument, and this pressure gave rise to the Concentric in 1968. The Concentric was so called because the float was at the bottom of the carburettor and the main jet projected down into the float chamber. The float chamber cover was fixed to the bottom of the main body, and the main body casting was designed so that the holes for the tuning screws could be drilled on either side – giving left or right handed models using the same casting. This cut costs and solved the access problems of the Monobloc.

The Concentric did have some problems on introduction – often bikes would stall when pulling up as the concentric design caused fuel starvation. The instrument also gained a reputation for rapid wear, especially between the slide and main body, which made it difficult to tune correctly when worn. On the plus side, the Concentric was cheap, relatively easy to maintain and did the job.

Frame and Swinging Arm

The frame of the Twenty-one was completely new and up to date, featuring swinging arm rear suspension from the start. The frame was made in two parts – a front loop and bolt-on rear sub-frame. The front loop was a semi-cradle design, made up from tubes and lugs brazed together – the traditional method of making frames in the 1950s, where steel tubes are brazed into cast iron lugs. It comprised a single front down tube, a large U-shaped tubular cradle supporting the bottom of the engine and single tube making up the top tube and seat tube, which ran from the headstock down to the rear of the engine cradle. The top tube was set lower than the headstock, and both it and the front tube were located in separate fittings in the headstock, and were reinforced with a welded bracing plate between them, giving rise to the headstock area being described as a 'swan's neck'. The lowered top tube meant that there was no need for a tunnel in the fuel tank, enabling its capacity to be increased without increasing its bulk. However, this design meant that the top of the headstock was unsupported. This was recognized by the factory, and the fuel tank had two supporting plates incorporated in it, and was bolted to the headstock and rear of the top tube to give the structure some additional strength.

The engine was bolted into the main loop of the frame at four points. The front fixing was provided using two engine plates, which bolted to a fixing on the down tube and to three points on the front of the crankcase – these bolts were also used to clamp the crankcases together at the front. The bottom fixing passed through a large lug on the base of the engine, and each of the lower cradle sides, and included spacers to ease the fitting of the engine. At the rear, the top of the integral gearbox was affixed to two small L-shaped engine plates, which were attached using two bolts to a lug on the seat tube. Finally, two stays were attached to the rocker box/head bolts to act as a head steady.

The rear sub-frame was of all-welded construction, and comprised a horizontal U-shaped seat support, with two supporting stays welded

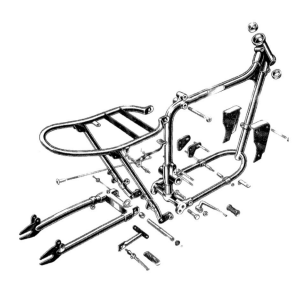

The 3TA frame was known as the 'swan's neck': while the frame was reinforced by the bolt-on fuel tank, the top of the headstock was not well supported.

While the Tiger Cub shared the 'swan's neck' of the 3TA, there are few other similarities, showing the 3TA frame to be a 'proper' design in its own right, not a modified Cub unit.

on approximately halfway along the seat support U tube. The front of the seat support (the open end of the U) bolted onto the top of the front loop's seat tube using a single stud passing through a lug. The two supporting stays bolted onto the end sides of the bottom cradle, locating on specially machined fixings. Two bolts secured each stay, one dedicated to the task and the other supporting the footrests, with the taper for the footrest mounts located on the front fixing of the stay. As the footrests were mounted on tapers, this gave a reasonable amount of adjustment.

The tubular swinging arm that held the rear wheel was pivoted on a ground hollow steel spindle, which was firmly located in a large lug on the seat tube of the main frame loop. The swinging arm bridge lugs carried two phosphor bronze bushes that provided a bearing surface for the swinging arm to pivot on the spindle. As the spindle was a drive fit in the frame lug, it should not move. Provision was made for lubricating the bushes through drillings in the spindle and a grease nipple in the frame. The spindle was retained in position by a rod that passed through the spindle that held retaining caps in place at both ends. Interestingly, in the original Twenty-one instruction manual, the life of the swinging arm spindle bushes was claimed to be approximately 20,000 miles (32,000km). While this was a good and reliable system, the outer ends of the swinging arm were not properly supported, so the arm could flex. The wheel spindle end of the swinging arm carried two Girling spring and damper units, the tops of which were connected to the rear sub-frame top rail.

The frame of the Twenty-one has been described by journalists as a development of the Triumph Tiger Cub frame, but had a number of significant differences. While the overall layout of both frames is similar, the Twenty-one's is considerably larger and more robust, as befitting the larger overall engine and the need to cope with some 50 per cent more power. The Twenty-one's front loop was of semi-cradle design, while the Tiger Cub was a single loop.

While both frames were of 'swan's neck' design, with a lowered top rail and reinforced fuel tanks to brace the headstock, the design of the headstocks differed significantly. The Tiger Cub had a single hole fixing for the front and top tube, with both ends of the tubes made into a 'D' section so they could share the single hole, while the Twenty-one had two fixing holes in the headstock, allowing the top and down tubes to be brazed into place separately. So while it can be seen that the Twenty-one's frame does contain some Tiger Cub DNA, there is no real substance to the theory it was just a beefed up Cub – there are enough unique features in the Twenty-one frame to show it was a well thought-out and well-engineered frame in its own right.

Frame and Swinging Arm Development

The frame and swinging arm of the 'C' Series underwent a period of intense development in the mid-1960s. Although the initial frame was pretty good, the unsupported headstock did lead to imprecise steering, and this problem was exaggerated as engine power was increased. Although the fuel tank was acted as a reinforcing strut, as it bolted onto the top of the headstock and the rear of the top tube, Triumph provided a bolt-on strut in 1960 for the US compctition machines. However, in 1965 (for the 1966 model year), Triumph did the right thing and produced a new frame front loop with fully triangulated support to the headstock. This was achieved by fitting a new brazed-in tube above the existing top tube, which meant new cast lugs for both the headstock and rear seat tube. The steering head angle was revised to 65 degrees. This effort certainly helped to stiffen the structure, but it was not good enough.

The third version of the original 3TA frame was introduced in 1966 for the 1967 model year, and while it was the same in principle as the 1965 frame, it had the thicker top tube running from the top of the headstock back to the seat tube, and the thinner triangulating tube positioned below – again both tubes being brazed into new lugs on the main loop. The fork stem angle was revised yet again to 62 degrees. This arrangement was to last until the final Daytona was produced in 1974.

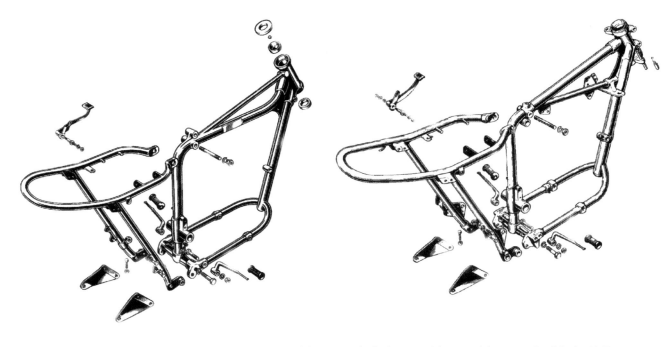

The next major change to the frame came in the 1966 model year, with a brazed-in strengthening top rail.

The final version of the original frame, introduced for the 1967 model year, had a new, thicker top rail and with a smaller-diameter reinforcing strut below it, and had lugs on the rear sub-frame to support the swinging arm pivot.

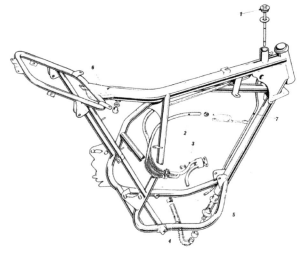

The 1967-onwards frame had lugs on the rear sub-frame that supported the ends of the swinging arm.

The TR5T frame was of all-welded construction, and carried the engine oil in the large-diameter top tube and the front down tube.

In 1967 Triumph also addressed the issue of the flexing of the swinging arm. In order to prevent the pivot from moving, the rear sub-frame had a pair of triangular lugs welded on, which carried bolts that fitted into the swinging arm pivot pin. This effectively prevented the pivot from flexing and sharpened up the handling.

The final years (1973–4) of the 'C' Range included the TR5T Adventurer/ Trophy Trail, which used a development of the BSA unit single frame. This was of all-welded construction, and carried its engine oil in its long top tube. (see Chapter 2). The swinging arm was carried in needle roller bearings, and the rear chain was adjusted by moving the whole wheel and swinging arm assembly in slots in the frame. Rear wheel alignment was assured using snail cam adjusters on the swinging arm pivot.

Front and Rear Suspension

The front forks that were fitted to the range were progressively developed to provide more rigidity and strength, along with better damping and travel.

The forks fitted to the first Twenty-one were internal spring, two-way damped units with steel sliders. The front wheel was fixed in place using caps that were secured to the bottom of the sliders with two bolts – a system that would be used on all subsequent models until the advent of the TR5T Adventurer/Trophy Trail. The top of the fork was completely concealed under the Triumph trademark nacelle, and steel covers protected the stanchions.

While the first T100SS lost the nacelle and gained rubber gaiters and a separate headlamp, the forks were still internal spring type, and were in essence the same as those fitted to the 3TA and 5TA. The speedometer (and optional rev counter) was mounted on a bracket that bolted onto the top yoke. The handlebars were rigidly mounted on to the top yoke with two bolt on lugs.

The 1964 T100SS saw the introduction of the heavyweight external spring forks to the 'C' range. The forks still provided two-way damping but had larger oil seal carriers to

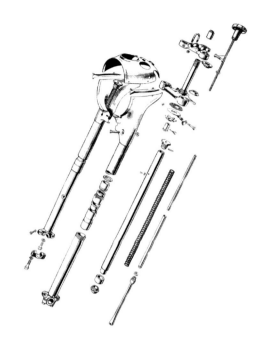

The 3TA front forks were two-way damped, with internal springs. The trademark Triumph nacelle tidied up the top end.

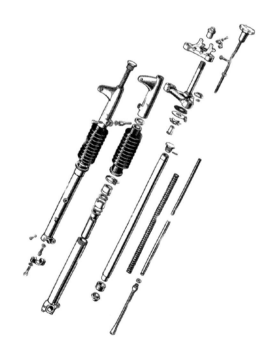

Early T100SS forks were restyled to give a sporty look, with rubber gaiters and a separate headlamp. Springs were still internal.

support the external springs. The speedometer and optional rev counter continued to be mounted on a bracket on the top yoke. The end of the nacelle was signified by a separate, chromed 7in (18cm) headlamp, which was carried on 'ears' fixed between both yokes. For 1968 the forks gained the two-way shuttle valve damping.

The forks saw little change after that, apart from widening of the yokes (from 6½in to 6¾in) to allow the fitting of a wider front tyre to allow in turn the fitting of the twin leading shoe front brake for 1969.

The final forks fitted to the TR5T Adventurer/Trophy Trail and the prototype T100D were the new corporate standard Ceriani type. These were developed from those used on the BSA works motocross bikes, and had lightweight alloy sliders and chromed steel stanchions.

There were no fork bushes as such, the stanchions running directly on the sliders. While this seems like a recipe for expensive replacement, in reality the system worked very well and few cases of worn-out sliders seem to occur. The front wheel had a fixed axle, which was fixed on to bottom of the slider using an alloy block, which was located on four studs. This fixing was claimed to give the forks such good rigidity that a brace at the top of the sliders was not needed. However, the forks could and did twist under pressure. The stanchions were exposed to the elements, so a tough rubber 'wiper' or dust excluder was fitted to the top of the slider to prevent the ingress of abrasive grime and water, and the alloy sliders had a polished finish. Oil seals were fitted below the dust excluders. The forks performed well, with dual damping, soft springing and around 5½–6in (14cm) depending on which specification you read) of travel. The head bearings were taper rollers as standard, a superior fitment to the ball races fitted on the previous frame.

Rear suspension on all models was provided by a swinging arm, which was sprung and damped by twin Girling type spring/shock absorbers that gave good control and adequate movement to the rear wheel.

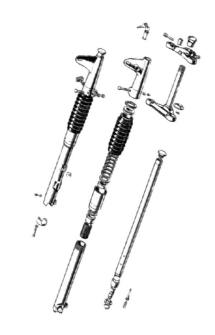

The later bikes had beefed-up forks, with external springs and separate headlamp. Two-way damping was provided by more efficient shuttle valves at the bottom of each stanchion.

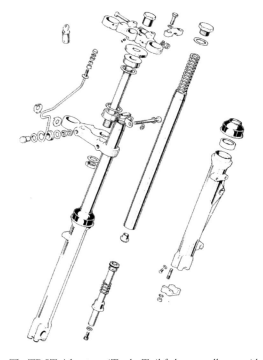

The TR5T Adventurer/Trophy Trail forks were all new, with alloy sliders, internal springs and wire mounts for the headlamp.

Brakes and Wheels

The Twenty-one was introduced with 7in-diameter (18cm) single leading shoe brakes, front and rear. They were up to the standards of the time, and offered reasonable stopping power. The front hub comprised a full-width cast iron drum with cooling fins on its perimeter, which was riveted to a pressed steel hub. The brake plate was alloy. The rear brake used identical brake shoes, and the cast iron brake drum was bolted onto the rear hub – although a quickly detachable (QD) hub was an optional extra. The QD hub allowed the removal of the wheel without disturbing the chain or brake. The rear brake drum was bolted to the swinging arm, and the wheel fitted into splines on the drum. Removing the wheel spindle and a spacer from the timing side of the wheel allowed the wheel to be removed. Galvanized spokes were used and 17in chromed steel rims at both ends complete the picture.

The rear brake remained a single leading shoe for the life of the range, but the front brake underwent some progressive development on the 500cc models.

For 1968, the Daytona gained a single leading shoe, 8in-diameter (20cm) front brake, as had been fitted to the 650s in 1967. This brake used a flange on the right-hand side of the hub to increase the drum area, giving an increase in braking power. This brake on the Daytona was changed to the 650's twin leading shoe variant in 1969. On the T100SS and T100C models the 7in (18cm) twin leading shoe brake with its flanged hub was adopted early in 1969 – as shown by the bike restored in the book, the earliest 1969 models however retained the single leading shoe brake! As with the 8in (20cm) hub, the flanged 7in (18cm) hub allowed a wider braking area than before, and the twin leading shoe operation gave a much more powerful braking effect. This brake was a small-

The 3TA and 5TA shared a 7in (18cm) front brake. This remained a standard fitment across the range until the introduction of the 8in (20cm) brake on the 1968 Daytona.

The rear brake was a 7in-diameter (18cm) item throughout the life of the range. Here is the version fitted to the 5TA.

The 8in (20cm) twin leading shoe front brake fitted to the 1969-onwards Daytona was considered by many to be Triumph's best ever drum brake.

er version of the more powerful 8in (20cm) twin leading shoe brake which was fitted to the Daytona, the 650cc bikes and the 750cc Trident. The 8in (20cm) version of this brake was the ultimate drum brake that Triumph produced, and it was powerful and smooth when properly set up.

When it was first introduced on the 650cc and 750 Trident in 1968, it had a long cable that swept down behind the wheel, and operated the brake mechanism from the lower rear of the brake plate. This led to a spongy operation, and the possibility of the cable catching on the front mudguard, so the 'bell crank' operation was introduced for 1969, where a shorter cable followed the line of the forks down to the brake back plate, which gave better feel and less spongy operation. This version of the brake was considered to be a better brake than the conical hub variant brought out in 1971, and equipped the Daytona through until 1974 when production ceased. Note that the 'C' Series never got the 1968 version of the 8in (20cm) TLS brake.

The TR5T Adventurer/Trophy Trail got the corporate conical hub brakes – an adequate 7in (18cm) single leading shoe at the rear, and an underwhelming single leading shoe 6in (15cm) unit on the front, which, while in keeping with the bike's offroad aspirations, proved to be inadequate on the road.

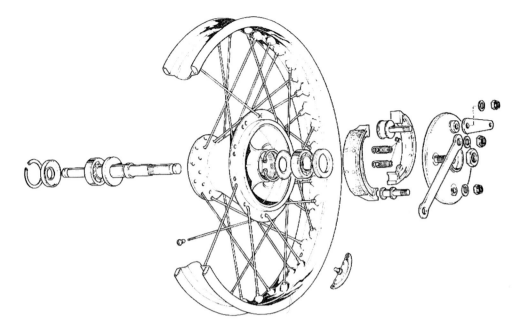

The TR5T Adventurer/Trophy Trail had a puny 6in (15cm) single leading shoe front brake. Good offroad, but not so good on the road.

Tinware

Full Enclosure – the Bathtub
The most striking feature of the Twenty-one was the enclosure of the rear half of the machine, which gave a smooth look to the machine and was a radical departure from the norm at the time. The styling was designed for a number of reasons: to get away from the 'nuts and bolts' appearance, to improve mud guarding, to make the machine easier to clean and to ape the appearance of the scooter that were so popular at the time.

Triumph's take on rear enclosure was comprehensive. The top half of the rear wheel and the midriff of the bike and were fully enclosed , with a cut-out each side exposing the wheel. In shape the enclosure resembled an upturned hip bath, giving rise to the not altogether complimentary nickname of 'the bathtub'. The enclosure was made from sheet steel, in two halves that were bolted together using six small bolts. The only

jarring note in the smoothly styled unit was the rear number plate, a standard Triumph item, which just did not look at all integrated. The bathtub had a chrome-plated casting of the model name written on each side – Twenty-one, Speed Twin or Tiger 100 in 'toothpaste script' mounted on each side of the enclosure below the nose of the seat.

Up front, the traditional Triumph nacelle adorned the front fork, enclosing the headlight, ammeter, switchgear and steering damper in a smooth package which extended down the fork legs in the form of stanchion covers. Beneath the nacelle the front mudguard was a large, heavily valanced unit with a flared-out rear. In profile its outline resembled a Roman helmet, and that is what it was nicknamed. The 650cc Thunderbird and the Tiger 110 'B' Series twins adopted the bathtub style in 1960, although the top-of-the-range sports 650s, the Bonneville and the Trophy set the trend for the years ahead with no enclosure and separate chromed headlamps rather than the traditional nacelle.

The bathtub was striking and not unattractive. Easy to clean, it also provided good weather protection and was complemented by the heavily valanced front mudguard.

The early bikes had the flange that joined the two halves of the bathtub together turned inside, making for a neat join but bad for access. The bathtub was changed in 1959 to have the flange outside, giving much easier access for maintenance.

The combination of the 'Roman helmet' front mudguard, nacelle and rear bathtub made a complete and coherently styled package that was both easy to clean and kept most of the road dirt off the rider.

The bathtub was used on the 3TA and the 5TA on their introduction. It was also used on the first year of the Tiger 100A on its introduction in 1960, and although the styling was questioned at the time as being not so appropriate to a more sporting model, the T100A continued with the bathtub until the replacement of the model with the T100SS with its partial enclosure in 1962.

The bathtub eventually disappeared at the end of the 1963 model year, when the 3TA and 5TA adopted the abbreviated bikini enclosures for the following year. While the bathtub was arguably a styling success at its introduction, it was looking old-fashioned and ungainly by the mid-1960s. Second and third owners of the bikes were pulling them off and discarding them, searching for a more modern look, and just as the more sporting models in the range went back to the naked look, so then did the tourers. The bathtub may have been practical and convenient, but motorcycling was changing, going from a necessity, for example a 'ride to work in the week and a sedate trip to the coast or out in the countryside at the weekend' to a leisure and 'youth' activity, and it had no part to play in the brave new world of the swinging sixties.

Partial Enclosure – the Bikini
The next stage on from Triumph's experiment with full enclosure was, not surprisingly, partial enclosure, with the introduction of the bikini

The Twenty-one, Speed Twin and Tiger 100 had their names written on their side panels in Triumph's 'toothpaste' script.

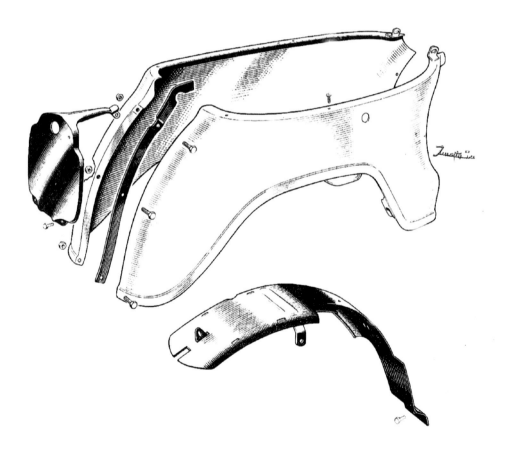

The full bathtub was an impressively large pair of panels.

Enclosure – The Great White Hope

Enclosure was the new trend for the British motorcycle manufacturers in the 1950s and early 1960s. Inspired by the scooter boom of the late 1950s, most of the major factories and many of the smaller marques introduced models with greater or lesser amounts of enclosure during this time. Triumph was the innovator in this trend with the Twenty-one in 1957, with Norton and the other UK factories (with the exception of BSA) following soon after. These designs ranged from simple covers over the engine and gearbox, through integrated rear enclosures like on the Twenty-one, to extremely enveloping bodywork, giving protection to both rider and machine.

The objective of all the extra tin was threefold: to provide weather protection, to give a modern stylish look, and to make the machine easy to clean. The introduction of these enclosures was met with some acclaim in the press, and was partially accepted by the buyers. However, while Edward Turner knew his market in the 1930s and 1940s he seems to have lost his touch by the end of the 1950s. The market was changing, both home and especially abroad (read USA, Triumph's major export market), and despite his frequent trips to the USA to study the market, Edward Turner

did not seem to perceive this. The motorcycle was no longer a ride-to-work machine, it was becoming a 'lifestyle' product. People bought them because they liked to ride, not because they had to ride, and although the British market was probably five to ten years behind the US, the trends were plain to see.

The ride-to-work market had largely been taken by the scooter. Many scooterists would probably never have bought a motorcycle but were attracted to scooters because they were simple to operate, and did not look or feel like motorcycles.

The best scooters (such as Vespa and Lambretta) were easy to ride, thanks to their flat 'floor' and the open space between the seat and handlebars, and easy to live with, with their hidden mechanicals, clean lines, good weather protection and stylish and attractive appearance. These machines were the result of a fully integrated design process, using monocoque construction to incorporate the frame and much of the bodywork in one single whole. This design integrity was reflected in the way they looked, in stark contrast to most of the enclosed motorcycles, where the additional bodywork was quite obviously tacked on to an existing design, and furthermore did

Enclosure was not limited to Triumph. Velocette made a bit of a half-hearted effort in the early 1960s with the V-Line models. On these the engine and gearbox were covered in glass-fibre panels and an aftermarket fairing was fitted.

not provide anywhere near the amount of weather protection provided by scooters. So, unless one wanted the performance of a larger machine, there was little point in going for an enclosed motorcycle rather than a scooter.

Perhaps the doomed attempt to introduce enclosure on mainstream motorbikes was a result of the aging decision-makers in the motorcycle industry. As one gets older, tastes change, and to the mature rider such enclosures did make sense. Maybe the management lost sight of what a major part of their market really wanted. To the younger rider – the buyer of the future – the enclosures were ugly and were the first thing to be removed. In the vast majority of cases they added weight and cut down on accessibility. Younger riders wanted sporty looks and never mind the practicality! The message slowly permeated through to the management at all of the British factories and enclosures disappeared through the 1960s.

RIGHT: Ariel (also part of the BSA/Triumph group) introduced their Leader in July 1958, with full enclosure and weather protection. It was probably a more effective set-up than the Triumph for all-year-round riding.

BELOW RIGHT: This 1959 5TA shows off Triumph's bathtub to full effect.

BELOW: Norton probably came closest to the Triumph way of doing things. Their rear enclosure (seen here on a 250cc Jubilee) was not as sleek as the Triumph's bathtub, but the large front mudguard certainly mimicked the Triumph effort.

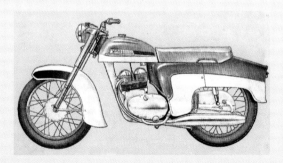

350 c.c. TRIUMPH TWENTY-ONE (3TA)

The bikini was a lot more visually appealing than the bathtub to the more sporting rider, who was beginning to dominate the marketplace in the mid-1960s.

350 c.c.   TRIUMPH TWENTY-ONE (3TA)

For 1965 the front mudguards were slimmed down, in line with the trend towards less enclosure.

enclosure on the T100S/S of 1962. The new rear enclosure was much smaller than the bathtub and only covered the midriff of the bike. The fairing was triangular in overall shape, following the frame line from the swinging arm pivot up to the top rear suspension, then running forwards, following the line of the seat base, finally dropping downwards from the seat nose back to the swinging arm pivot.

A styling crease followed the line of the front and top edge, and, as with the previous bathtub, the model name was written in a chromed 'toothpaste' script on the middle of the panel. The new panelling was accompanied on the T100SS by a separate chromed headlamp, matching speedometer and rev counter mounted on a plate on the fork top yoke and slim sports mudguards. All in all the appearance of the bike was much more sporting than with the bathtub, but it did retain some of the bathtub's practicality in terms of weather protection and 'cleanability'. The T90 adopted the look from its introduction in 1963, and the 3TA and 5TA also moved over to the new partial enclosure in 1964, but retained the larger 'Roman helmet' front mudguard and nacelle.

The bikini survived for some years, but the T100S/S and T90 lost theirs in 1964 and the 3TA and 5TA went 'naked' in their last year, in 1966. Bikini style was also adopted by the 650cc Thunderbird in 1963 and lasted until 1965 on that model, but was not used on the 650cc Trophy or Bonneville.

Naked

The US market was the first to dispense with the enclosures with the introduction of the TR5A/R for 1961. This model had no side panel on the drive side, just an exposed battery and air cleaner. Intended for on/offroad sport, it also featured a separate chromed 6in (15cm) headlamp, a speedometer mounted on the fork yoke and slim mudguards.

The first models to dispense with enclosure entirely in the UK market were the 1964 Tiger 90 and Tiger 100SS. These went back to the classic Triumph look, with a handsome rounded fuel tank, exposed oil tank on the timing side and matching side panel on the drive side, and slim painted mudguards.

The nacelle was replaced with a 7in (18cm) chromed bullet-shaped headlamp, with the matching speedometer and tachometer mounted on a bracket on the top yoke. The rest of the models in the range eventually followed suit, with the 3TA and 5TA dropping their partial enclosure for 1966, but retaining the nacelle until their eventual demise that year. The T100 range that ran on to the end of the line in the 1970s never returned to an enclosed look, but kept the naked look that became the classic Triumph look through to the present day.

Electrics

The electrics of the Twenty-one reflected the changes being made throughout the British motorcycle industry at the time. Moving away from the mechanically complex and expensive DC dynamo/magneto systems, the Twenty-one had a Lucas 6v alternator fitted inside the primary chain case. This provided 60 watts of power, in a package that was easier to drive and lighter than the old dynamos. Probably more significant for Triumph (and its customers), was that the alternator was cheaper than the dynamo.

The magneto was sent the same way as the dynamo, with ignition being coil based and reliant on a charged battery. Voltage regulation and battery charging was carried out using a fiendishly complicated combined ignition and light switch (Lucas PRS8) to switch in extra alternator coils as the load was increased. To quote from the *Triumph Twenty-one Instruction Manual No 1* (published in March 1957):

The alternator stator carries three pairs of series connected coils, one pair being permanently connected across the rectifier bridge. The purpose of this latter pair is to provide some degree of charging current for the battery whenever the engine is running. Connections to the remaining coils vary according to the positions of the lighting and ignition switch controls. When no lights are in use, the alternator output from the battery

For 1965 Triumph followed their stance in the US market and dropped the enclosures
from the UK-market sports models. Here is a 1965 T100SS in all its naked glory.

500 c.c. TRIUMPH TIGER 100 (T100S/S)

The factory shot of the 1965 T100SS shows how well styled the bikes were without any enclosures.

However, there was not much change to the styling from 1965 onwards, other than changing the colour, as this 1970 Daytona shows.

charging coils is regulated to a minimum by the inter-action of the rotor flux set up by the current flowing in the short circuited coils. In the "PILOT" position these latter coils are disconnected and the regulating fluxes are consequently reduced. The alternator output therefore increases and compensates for the additional parking light load. In the "HEAD" position, the alternator output is further increased by the connection of all three pairs of coils in parallel.

A complex explanation for a complex system! The main point is that there is no active regula-tion of the current generated, so the battery is either being overcharged or undercharged at any one time. But, to give it its due, the system did seen to work reasonably well, and if the battery did go flat, there was always the 'EMG' setting on the ignition switch. This, again to quote the *Instruction Manual*:

> With this circuit the contact breaker is arranged to open when the alternating current in the windings reaches a maximum. The ignition coil primary wind-ing and the contact breaker are connected in series. When the contacts separate, H.T. current is induced in the coil secondary windings, thus producing a spark at the pug. Since, with the ignition switch at "EMG" and the engine running, the battery receives a charg-ing current, the battery voltage soon begins to rise. The rising voltage opposes the alternator, gradually effecting a reduction in the energy available for trans-fer to the coil. In the event of a rider omitting to return the ignition key from position "EMG" to posi-tion "IGN" this reduction in spark energy will cause misfiring to occur and will remind the rider to switch over to normal running.

Once the system got a bit old, with corrosion in the switch and a battery beyond its best, the charging/ignition/lighting system would become unreliable, due to the inherent complex-ity of the system, the less than high-quality com-ponents used and the lack of any 'active' voltage regulation. However, if kept in good condition the system does work!

There was one set of ignition points housed in a distributor situated behind the cylinder block,

driven from a spur gear on the inlet camshaft. A rotor arm within the distributor directed the HT current from the coil to the appropriate HT lead – a system used on most cars of the day. The whole top of the distributor was encased in a rubber moulding to keep the water out and the sparks in. While the system worked well when new, wear would render exact timing problemat-ical. The skew gears that drove the distributor from the inlet camshaft could wear and develop backlash, while the distributor body had bearings to support the shaft that drove the advance retard unit and the contact breaker points cam – all of which could and did wear. Again, the distributor was a complex mechanical device with many potential points of failure, so was not ideal.

The distributor on the early machines was complex and prone to wear, and was prone to backlash and hence inaccurate timing when the drive gears and bearing started to wear.

The rest of the electrics were the norm for the time, a no-frills system of headlamp, ammeter, tail light, brake light and horn – no warning lights or indicators in those days. However, the ammeter was used to monitor the health of the system, and to ensure the battery was getting some charge.

In 1960 the sporting models in the range, the T100A, TR5A and TR5AR, were equipped with the Lucas Energy Transfer system. This system was designed to allow a bike to be run without a bat-tery, and relied on the precise positioning of the alternator rotor and stator to provide a maximum energy pulse of electricity to the coil when the contact breaker points operated. While the system did work, it was very sensitive to any changes to its set-up (such as the position of the alternator rotor relative to the stator, and the points gap), and could not tolerate any wear in the components that made up the system (such as the distributor). The system proved to be troublesome in service, probably because it was far to complex to be ser-viced 'in the field', and was quietly dropped mid-way through the 1961 model year.

Development of the electrical system followed the 'standard' British bike line – with the advent of alternators there was the prospect of going to 12v systems, which gave better lighting and

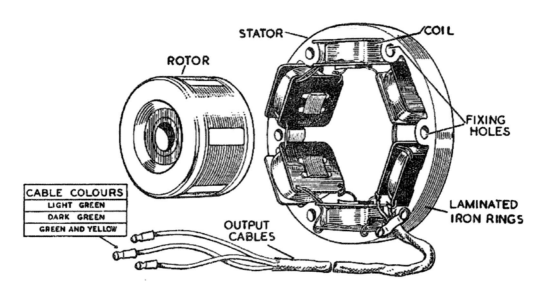

The RM13/15 alternator as fitted to the 3TA was a neat design. The
most significant design change made during its life was to encapsulate
the coils in resin so they could survive in the primary chain case.

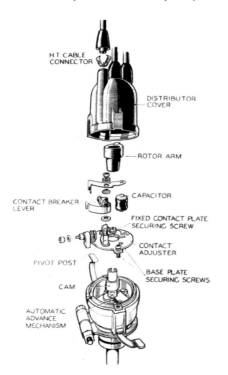

**12-volt equipment on all twin cylinder
models. Raising hinged twin seat gives
easy access to the two 6-volt batteries,
and to the neat tool tray.**

The distributor worked well when new, but wear in its various
mechanisms could lead to poor performance.

The first 12v systems had twin 6v batteries in an enlarged carrier,
and the Zener diode heat sink tucked neatly out of the cooling
slipstream behind the side panel.

reliability. The arrival of the Lucas Zener Diode provided a solid state voltage regulator, and set the scene for reliable and simple electrical systems for the range from the mid-1960s.

The 'C' Series range went over to 12v for 1966, and the improvement in both performance and reliability was noted by the press at the time. The system was simple, and removed the need for the complex PRS8 switch and multiple wires from the alternator. Equipment fitted remained much the same as before, but with the gradual addition of warning lights for oil pressure and main beam in the headlamp shells.

The last major change to the models electrical system came in 1971, when flashing direction indicators became standard, along with alloy handlebar switches integrated into the brake and clutch levers. The ergonomics of these switches came in for some criticism, as they were a bit of a stretch for people with smaller hands. The switches themselves supported a headlamp flasher and kill switch as well as horn, main/dip beam and indicators, so represented quite a leap in sophistication for the electrics compared to the pre-1971 machines.

Instruments and Controls

The Twenty-one's instrumentation was not particularly comprehensive, comprising just a nacelle-mounted Smiths chronometric speedometer and ammeter, but was broadly in line with the competition and the standards of the day.

The speedometer had a milometer to record total mileage, and a separate trip meter which could be reset to record trip mileage. Along with the speedometer and ammeter, the combined light and ignition switch and the steering damper now also occupied the nacelle, which resulted in a clean, uncluttered display for the rider.

The only other form of instrumentation was the mechanical oil pressure indicator, situated on the front of the engine and all but invisible to the rider when seated on the machine. Also used on the 500cc and 650cc pre-unit engines, it comprised a mechanical plunger that protruded out

from the oil pressure release switch if the oil pressure was OK. On the earlier, pre-unit Triumph engines, the indicator was positioned at the bottom of the timing cover at right angles to the engine so the indicator protruded outwards, and was visible to the rider if he or she looked down. On the Twenty-one, the indicator was placed on the front of the engine, and was almost impossible to see when the machine was being ridden. However, the oil system was pretty reliable, and failures when riding were rare.

A combined horn and dip switch was fitted to the left hand handlebar. There were no warning lights on the first Twenty-ones.

As the range developed, the instrumentation became more comprehensive. Once the nacelle was lost on the T100S/S of 1962, the speedometer was mounted on a separate bracket on the top yoke which was isolated from vibration by rubber bushes.

A tachometer (rev counter) was introduced as an optional extra on the T100, and was mounted alongside the speedometer on an extended bracket. Both instruments were illuminated when the lights were turned on.

The speedometer and tachometer (when fitted) were Smith Chronometric types up to 1963, then Smiths Magnetic type from 1964, although police machines continued to be equipped with specially calibrated Smiths Chronometric instruments.

The lights were operated by a three-position rotary switch (off/pilot/main) which was mounted on the left-hand side panel until 1967, when it was moved to the headlamp shell. The light switch then changed to the Lucas 35710 toggle type on the headlamp in 1968. The dip/main beam and horn was operated by a cheap-looking, chrome-plated, clamp-on switch on the left-hand (clutch) handlebar. This was an area that the Japanese with their cast alloy combined switch units were streets ahead of Triumph (and the other British factories). Triumph would not produce a decent integrated alloy handlebar switch until 1971.

On the electrical front, the warning lights for ignition (green) and main beam (red) were

The nacelle gave a neat and uncluttered appearance to the fork top. An ammeter, ignition/light switch, steering damper and speedometer were all a rider needed!

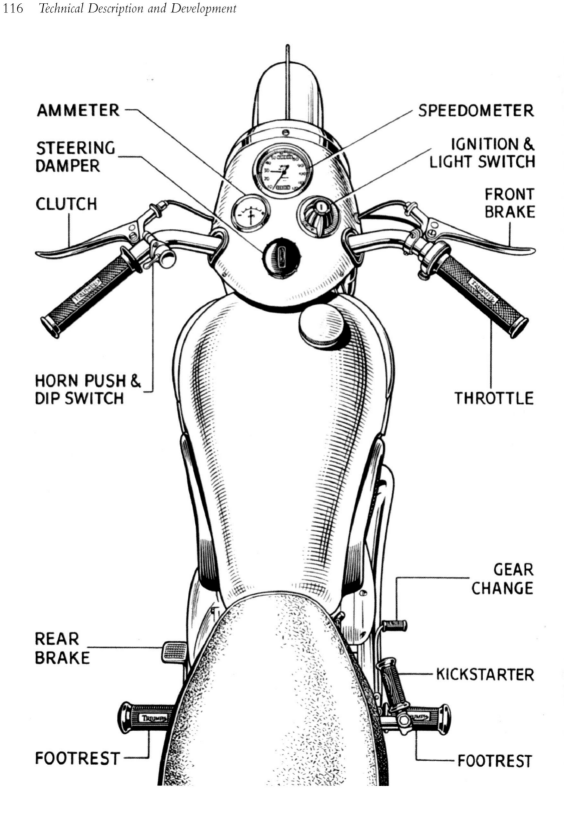

AMMETER

STEERING
DAMPER

CLUTCH

SPEEDOMETER

IGNITION &
LIGHT SWITCH

FRONT
BRAKE

HORN PUSH &
DIP SWITCH

THROTTLE

GEAR
CHANGE

REAR
BRAKE

KICKSTARTER

FOOTREST

FOOTREST

standardized for US models in 1967 (up to engine/frame number H49833 to H57082) and mounted in the separate headlight, but were optional for home and export models for some years previously. Home models adopted the same standard warning lights in 1968. From mid-1968 (engine/frame number H65573), the warning lights were revised, when the home and US T100R Daytona was equipped with a red oil pressure warning light and a green high-beam light.

The next major change to the instruments came in 1971 (engine/frame number KE00001 onwards) with the introduction of flashing indicators and new integrated handlebar switches/control levers. The flashers needed an amber warning light, and this was positioned in the headlamp, along with the red oil light and green main beam warning light. The bikes received new handlebar switchgear, which comprised alloy castings with the handlebar lever piv-

ABOVE: *The T100C's single speedometer was mounted on a central bracket on the fork top yoke. The two-tone grey face on the instrument was used up to 1970.*

OPPOSITE: *The controls of the 1957 3TA were simple and somewhat sparse!*

BELOW: *The dual instruments, speedometer and tachometer, were mounted on a rubber-mounted bracket on the fork top yoke. From the middle of the 1970 model year the black face replaced the earlier grey.*

The final Lucas type of handlebar switch fitted to the Daytona came in for some criticism because of the reach needed to operate it.

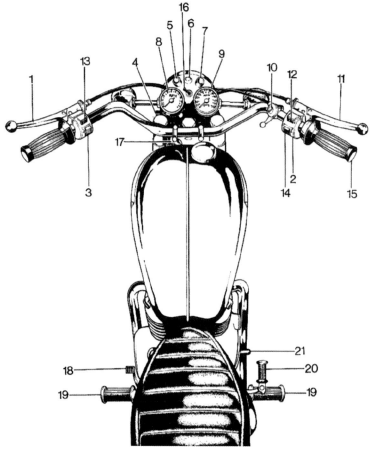

The last of the Daytonas were not so different in control layout from the original 3TA.

KEY:

1	Clutch Lever
2	Horn Push
3	Direction Indication Switch
4	Ignition Switch
5	Oil Pressure Warning Light (Red)
6	Direction Indicator Warning Light (Amber)
7	Main Beam Warning Light (Green)
8	Tachometer
9	Speedometer
10	Air Control Lever
11	Front Brake Lever
12	Headlamp Flasher
13	Kill Button
14	Dip Switch
15	Throttle Control
16	Lighting Switch
17	Parking Lock
18	Rear Brake Lever
19	Footrest
20	Kickstarter Pedal
21	Gearchange Pedal

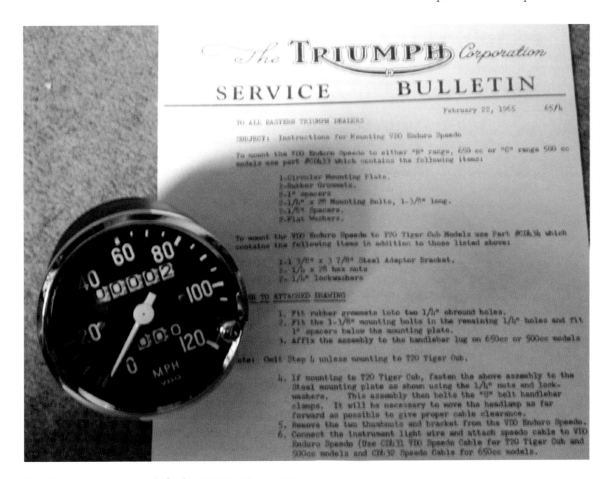

The VDO speedometer was only fitted to 1966/1967 competition models. An original would have a 'Triumph' logo on the face.

ots on the front and a standardized switch console on the rear. Each console had a central toggle switch which was either two-position (up/down) for dip/main or three-position (up/off/down) for the indicators. In addition there were two press and hold buttons above and below the toggle switch.

For 1971 the right-hand switch toggle operated the indicators, with the toggle being operated up for left and down for right, while the top press button operated the ignition kill function. The left-hand cluster's toggle operated the dip/main beam; the lower push button operated horn and the upper operated the headlamp flasher. The bikes lost the ammeter at this time, and the new handlebar switches came in for

some criticism for not being as easy to use as equivalent Japanese units.

One aside was the fitting of speedometers manufactured by German firm VDO for the 1966–7 T100C models. The VDO Enduro Speedo was the subject of a Triumph Corporation Service Bulletin, dated 22 February 1965, which gave instructions on how to use a mounting bracket kit (part number CD433) to fit the instrument. The speedo was the same diameter as the Smiths speedos, but its body was much deeper than the Smith's magnetic type. The VDO speedo also had a trip meter with the reset knob placed on the face of the instrument, making it easier to get at than the Smiths side-mounted version.

4 Competition History

The C Series twins showed much potential for competition right from their introduction. The two main areas that they competed in was scrambles (or moto cross) and road racing. With their light weight, good power and easy-to-tune motors, the bikes were competitive in both areas through the 1960s. There were also attempts to use the 3TA in trials, where it achieved some limited success. However, there were two arenas where the bikes really shone – at the US's premier road race, Daytona, and in the International Six Days Trials, the mainly European on/offroad event that tested bikes and riders to the limit.

Daytona – 1966 and 1967

Probably the 'C' Series Triumph's best run of racing success was its performance at the USA's prestigious Daytona 200 races. The Daytona circuit in Florida hosted what many people considered to be the premier races of the US competition season; it was run on the beach and a parallel road, giving a probably unique on/offroad circuit. For 1961 a new circuit was introduced, the Daytona International Speedway, which removed the famous beach section, making it a real road race circuit. The first Daytona 200-mile (320km) race at the new circuit saw Don Burnett on a Triumph T100 achieving a second place. The bike was prepared by Cliff Guild, a Tri-Cor employee. In the light of this achievement – equalling Triumph's previous best at the races, when Hugh McAffee piloted a pre-unit T100 to a second place – Triumph made a determined attempt to win the following year. Tri-Cor sponsored Burnett with a T100, again prepared and tuned by Guild, and in a thrilling race Burnett eventually won the race, finishing a mere 12ft (3.6m) ahead of a Matchless G50 500cc ohc single ridden by Dick Mann.

This victory led to what was the 'C' Series Triumph's most significant road racing success, with Tri-Cor- and Meriden-prepared bikes winning the Daytona 200-mile National Championship Road Race in 1966 and 1967.

The 1966 bikes were based on the production roadsters, but featured significant changes. Doug Hele's experimental department at Meriden prepared six bikes in total and took

In action the 1969 T100C was an excellent trail bike, and had good road manners as well. This is a 1969 brochure shot.

Buddy Elmore, mounted on a 500cc Triumph, wins Daytona in 1966.

five to Daytona, while Tri-Cor prepared a number of their own bikes.

The Meriden bikes featured new frames, which, while following the production model's layout, were made using Reynolds 531 tubing, which was stronger and lighter than the standard tubing, and had the seat height lowered by 1½in (4cm). The swinging arm pivot featured external bracing, and the area around the headstock was strengthened, giving better handling. New, centre-mounted oil tanks were made, somewhat ungainly BSA alloy fuel tanks were fitted and the engines were tuned and modified to give both reliability and performance.

Another shot of Buddy Elmore on the 1966 Daytona-winning Triumph.

The works Triumph ridden by Buddy Elmore in 1966 was based closely on the production T100. Note the oil cooler on the front of the engine, plumbed into the return side, the special points housing and non-standard carburettors.

The engine benefited from a new cylinder head, with the valve angle reduced from 45 degrees to 39 degrees, a redesigned combustion chamber and larger inlet valves. Twin Amal Grand Prix (GP) carburettors were fitted on rubber tubes, and the ignition was provided by on/off Lucas racing Energy Transfer units, driven from the exhaust camshaft to give precise ignition timing at high revs. Magnesium outer engine covers helped to keep the weight down. The exhaust system was a high-level twin silencer system, with both exhaust pipes routed over the left-hand side above the primary chain case, and equipped with two racing megaphones. The Meriden bikes produced 46.5bhp at 8,200rpm.

The practice for the race showed the Meriden bikes to be fragile – several engines broke their connecting rods, and tappet blocks, specially made for the engines in alloy, worked loose, wrecking camshafts. Eventually, Buddy Elmore and Dick Hammer started the race on a Meriden-prepared bike, while Gary Nixon set off on a Guild-prepared Tri-Cor machine. In the race, Hammer's engine failed after seven laps and Nixon's rear tyre was punctured on the forty-fifth lap. Elmore's bike held together for the full fifty-three laps, and he won with a new record speed of 96.38mph(155.08km/h).

The bikes' performance in 1966 lead to the adoption of the name 'Daytona' for the top-of-the-range twin carburettor sports model in the 1967 range.

Building on the somewhat fraught experiences of 1966, Triumph's experimental

Drive-side view of the 1966 Daytona-winning T100. The high-level exhaust increased ground clearance. The BSA alloy tank was not a good fit to the seat.

OPPOSITE: *A shot of the Triumph pits during practice for Daytona in 1967.*

The winning Triumph team at Daytona 1967: team manager Rod Coats is first left, rider Ron Grant second left, wearing the cap.

department set to work to solve the problems for the 1967 race.

Meriden prepared six bikes for the race. The engines were refined, with a new cylinder head with squish bands and lightened valve gear. The problematical connecting rods were replaced with stronger items and the camshafts were 'hotter'. The breathing system was improved and the engines produced 48.5bhp at 8,700rpm – not a great increase on the 1966 units, but the engines had much better mid-range power. A new close ratio gearbox cluster enabled the increased power to be used, and a new exhaust system, with the right-hand pipe sweeping under the engine gave much better access to the engine without compromising ground clearance. The front forks featured new internals, with a shuttle valve at the bottom of the stanchion giving two-way damping. A large 210mm diameter Fontana front brake unit was fitted. This brake was a double-sided unit, with four leading shoes, and provided much greater braking power than the previous year's production-based unit. A nicely styled glass-fibre fuel tank replaced the BSA alloy unit.

Practice for the race went smoothly, and at the end of the race Gary Nixon was first and Buddy Elmore second. All six factory bikes finished, with five placed in the top ten finishers, and the previous year's record was broken with a new race speed record of 98.22mph (158.04km/h). All in all this was a brilliant performance from what was essentially a modified roadster – albeit with some exotic factory parts and excellent preparation.

A postscript to the Daytona victories was the use of the works Daytona racers in Europe. Ray Knight won the 500cc class in the production TT on the Isle of Man in 1968, and Percy Tait, one of Meriden's testers and a mean road racer, used a 500 in 1969 in some international events, with moderate success.

His best outing was in the Belgian Grand Prix, where he came in second, just behind the works 500 MV Agusta works bike ridden by Agostini.

THE 200 MILE AMA CLASSIC WINNER

DAYTONA

...as a Meriden-built Triumph
...r 100 which carried Texan
...dy Elmore to victory in the 1966
... mile National Championship
...d Race at Daytona, Florida.

...race is America's toughest
... racing event of the com-
...on year, and Elmore set up a
...shing new race record of
...82 m.p.h., almost two m.p.h.
...on the previous record –
...this on a machine basically
...ar to any T100 in your local
...r's showroom.

*Triumph won at Daytona in 1966 and let the world know with this
full-page spread in the 1967 brochure.*

Production and Clubman Racing

The 'C' Series Triumph proved itself to be a competitive machine in international competition by winning both at Daytona and in numerous ISDTs, but it also helped to support a flourishing private racing effort across the world. In all types of sport, from road racing to offroad trials and scrambles the bike (or just the engine) showed itself to be cheap and easy to tune and make into a competitive mount.

Production racing events such as the Brands Hatch 500-miler (800km) in 1968 saw wins for the 500cc Triumph ridden by Peter Butler. Interestingly the bike used was Daytona-based, but sported the 8in (20cm) twin leading shoe front brake fitted to the T120 Bonneville.

Other modifications include Thruxton-type silencer, again off the 650cc bikes, a non-standard large-capacity oil tank and alloy fuel tank.

International Six Days Trials (ISDT)

Triumph have a long and illustrious history of competing and winning the International Six Days Trials. The ISDT was an event held yearly, and was a severe test of both man and machine. The trial was just that – an extended test of the man and machine, featuring timed and observed rides both on- and off-road, and performance tests.

The whole event was run over six days and nights, and the rider had to do all his own maintenance, using only tools and spares carried on

ABOVE: *The works Daytonas continued to be used on the European circuits after Daytona. Here is Percy Tait on a works Daytona in 1969.*

LEFT: *The T100C was a very slim bike, which helped enormously with its offroad ability. Here the restored 1969 model shows how slim it really is.*

OPPOSITE TOP: *Peter Butler cornering hard on a Daytona at the Brands Hatch 500-mile race in May 1968. He was the 500cc class winner.*

OPPOSITE BOTTOM: *Peter Butler's Daytona, the 500cc class winner at the Brands Hatch 500-miler in May 1968. Note the large-capacity oil tank, 1968 twin leading shoe front brake and Triumph T120 Thruxton-style silencers.*

ABOVE: The Boyer Team racing at Brands Hatch, Easter 1968. Dave Nixon is on a T100 Daytona (18) while team mate Peter Butler is on a T120R Bonneville. BELOW: Mick Chatterton riding a Daytona in the Production TT in the late 1960s.

the bike. Outside help could result in disqualification. The event was open to teams and individuals, and Triumph was a keen competitor, as the tough regime was an ideal shop window for Triumph's products. During the late 1950s and 1960s Triumph used both the 'C' Series and 'B' Series twins, and the Tiger Cub to compete the yearly event, with considerable success. For example, in the 1964 ISDT, Triumph twins won gold medals, and a manufacturers' team award. All through the 1960s Triumph twins kept on winning the event, and Triumph continued to enter works teams. However, as the BSA/Triumph conglomerate plunged into the red at the end of the 1960s, works support for the ISDT was withdrawn. The British motorcycle industry formed

a consortium in 1970 to provide a British team, and turned to Triumph 'C' Series-engined, Cheney-framed bikes to do the business.

The last Triumph works involvement in the ISDT came in the 1973 event. The 1973 ISDT was held in the Berkshire Mountains of Massachusetts in the USA. Bert Hopwood tasked Pete Colman of the then Triumph importer BSACI with preparing eight TR5T Adventurers for entry in the event by both US and English teams. Bob Tryon, Triumph's top service man, managed the Triumph Technical centre at Duarte. The bikes were meticulously prepared to counter any possibility of mechanical failure. The engines were blueprinted, and half were bored out to 504cc to enter the above 500cc category. The

Triumph rider in the 1966 ISDT held in Sweden.

Eric Cheney

Eric Cheney was a well-known and skilled scrambler star during the 1950s and had considerable success. After a prolonged illness in 1961, he decided to retire from racing to concentrate on frame building and preparing bikes for other riders. Starting off in his home workshop, he was soon successful enough to move to bigger premises and employ several workers.

Eric started off building frames for the BSA unit singles, initially in the early 1960s for the 250cc engines, and as the works scramblers were developed, he kept in touch with the competition shop.

Alongside the BSA engined frames, Eric built frames for the Triumph 'C' Series through the 1960s and early 1970s, although he did use various other engines for the scramblers and also built trials and road racing frames. The 'standard' frames for the Triumph engine were single down tube and had the oil contained in frame from the word go. This production single down tube frame was much easier to build than the twin down tube version.

The Cheney frame-building philosophy was to build on experience. Having ridden many works and production machines, Eric Cheney knew what could and did happen to the frames, and ensured that these faults were designed out in his frames, working on the principle that prevention was better than cure. His philosophy was to make the frames as strong and as light as possible, and he used the best materials around. During the 1960s and 1970s this meant using either Reynolds 531 or T45 steel tube. Nowadays Cheney frames, still built by Eric's son Simon, continue in this tradition, but use totally up to date materials such as top grade 4130 steel tube.

Eric Cheney started building frames for the 350cc and 500cc 'C' Series Triumph engines around 1965,

The original Cheney duplex down tube frame fitted with a T100 engine. Note the welded-on ears on the down tubes that protect the crankcases.

The swinging arm pivot is properly supported in the Cheney frame.
Footrest hangers clamp onto the lower frame tubes and support
folding footrests.

A Cheney-framed bike can fly. This is Malcolm Dearn leaping an early
Cheney-framed Triumph at Hollister.

Eric Cheney *continued*

using the first of the points in side engines. He continued to build frames for the engines all through the 1960s and 1970s, and many of the frames were exported to the USA, where they proved very popular in offroad sports.

The frames were identical to the frames produced for the BSA singles, with a single down tube (although the original team bikes were twin down tubes). The bikes tended to run better using a single carburettor. Simon never used to like riding the Triumph-engined bikes – mainly because the lack of engine braking did not suit his riding style. The Triumph could be made to run quicker than a BSA, but it was different and it was generally acknowledged that it was more difficult to ride a Triumph-engined bike fast than an equivalent BSA-engined one.

In 1970 Cheney supplied six 'C' Series Triumph-powered bikes for use by the British ISDT team. By this time the factory was not interested in supporting the ISDT, and so it was down to a group of dealers to put together a team. Eric Cheney got the contract to provide the bikes. The team comprised John Pease, Mick Williamson, John

Giles, Malcolm Rathmell, Jim Sandiford, and rider/manager Ken Heanes

As the 1970s progressed, Cheney moved away from the four-strokes that were becoming increasingly uncompetitive in the scramble market, and embraced the two-stroke, building his frames to take engines from other manufacturers and maintaining his reputation for producing competitive bikes.

The firm started producing BSA- and Triumph-engined bikes again in 1988 as the market for classic bikes and classic scramblers started to emerge. The market developed from people asking for their Cheney classic scramblers to be 'reverse modified' to make then eligible for classic events, to requests for batches of copies of works-type frames. Cheney saw that demand for his classic frames was on the up, and recommenced building the scrambler frames, including those for the BSA unit singles.

Eric Cheney sadly passed away in 2001, but the company is still family run today by Eric's son Simon. The firm still makes frames following the Cheney philosophy and offers frame kits, rolling chassis or complete frames,

The UK 1970 ISDT team mounted on their Cheney Triumphs. Left to right: John Pease, Mick Williamson, John Giles, Malcolm Rathmell, Jim Sandiford and rider/manager Ken Heanes.

in scrambles, ISDT or road trim. Engines catered for include the BSA unit singles from 250cc to 500cc, and unit and pre-unit Triumph 350cc, 500cc and 650cc engines. Pre-unit singles from BSA, Ariel, AJS and many other makes are also available. Renovations of previous customer's bikes are offered, and the company stock or can supply spares for all of the firm's products. Trading as Intermoto, Simon Cheney operates from Unit 3, Potters Industrial Park, Coxmoor Close, Aldershot Road, Church Crookham, Fleet, Hampshire GU52 6EU, and can be contacted on 01252 613680.

Over in the USA, long-term Triumph dealer and rider Bud Ekins has a Cheney Triumph in his back yard.

Rear view of the 1970 ISDT team Cheney Triumphs.

The 1970 British ISDT team mounted on their Cheney Triumphs. Left to right: John Pease, Mick Williamson, John Giles, Malcolm Rathmell, Jim Sandiford and rider/manager Ken Heanes.

The basis for the 1973 ISDT bikes was the Triumph TR5T Adventurer/Trophy Trail. This is a 1974 variant, virtually identical to the 1973 model.

heavy steel side panels were discarded and replaced with leather screens, which were held in place with Velcro. The standard steel mudguards replaced with plastic items. All the electrics were duplicated, with most of the components located under the right-hand side leather cover for easy access. A siamesed exhaust system was routed under the engine and exited through a short silencer mounted just above the swinging arm on the timing side. The front forks were Spanish Betor, allowing for a quickly detachable front wheel using a Rickman front hub. The dual seat incorporated a zip-up tool pouch, and there were many other detail modifications, such as running the rear brake pedal over the footrest, welding a tube to the lower frame cradle to protect the primary chain case, and deleting the battery, running instead on the Lucas ET system. The lights ran

directly from the alternator, with the standard chrome headlamp on the British team's machines and a rubber one on the US team's.

The weight of the ISDT bikes was reduced from the standard 340lb (154kg) to about 306lb (138kg), but were still significantly heavier than the Husqvarna, Maicio and CZ two-strokes that were dominating the competition at the time. All this detailed preparation was rewarded when the teams won three gold medals and one silver, with the English team taking a silver medal after coming behind the Czechoslovakian team riding CZs. The only significant failure was one of the American bikes breaking its forks (which were Spanish Betors not Triumph!) – a testament to the skills of the team doing the preparation and the strength and suitability of the BSA/Triumph hybrid that was the Adventurer.

5 Owning and Riding – Yesterday and Today

A 'C' Series twin makes a great introduction to classic riding, or a practical classic for the vertically challenged! The bikes are light, manoeuvrable and offer good performance, handling, road holding and economy. The electrics range from adequate in the early 6v models to good and reliable in the later 12v models – with the possible exception of Energy Transfer-equipped models. However, early and ET equipped models are easily updated and improved. Spares availability across the range is good, although, in common with most other classics, the early tinware can be hard to find. Mechanical spares, on the other hand, are easy to locate, and there are many upgrades, such as electronic ignition, modern tyres and solid state electrical components that can be used to discreetly improve the models. While the later frames are excellent, the earlier ones are perfectly fine for everyday use; a Daytona will provide the ultimate performance, but even a Twenty-one offers performance adequate to keep up with today's traffic, though it may be advisable to avoid motorways!

The following sections give some hints and tips on getting and keeping a 'C' Series twin running well, and also interviews a number of past and present owners of the bikes.

The 1965 T100 was a good-looking bike, especially with the small US fuel tank.

Hints and Tips

Oil Filter

The somewhat rudimentary oil filtration system can benefit from a full flow oil filter. With only two coarse gauze filters, in the sump and the oil tank and the crankshaft sludge trap, the filtration system is firmly rooted in the dark ages when monograde oils were changed in the spring and autumn, with 50 grade for the summer (hotter) season and 30 grade for the winter (colder) season. The monogrades of the 1950s did not contain detergents, which modern oils do. This meant that any particles in the oil would not be suspended in it but would 'fall out' of the oil at standstill, giving rise to a sludge that would settle in the oil tank, and would only be flushed out at the regular oil change. Modern multigrade (and some monograde) oils will have added detergents that carry the particles around in suspension and

a full flow filter is needed to get rid of them. This should be plumbed into the return side of the oil system, so it catches any bits and pieces that engine wear produces, and catches it before it gets into the oil tank and ends up recirculated through the engine.

Ignition

Electronic ignition is a real boon, with major advantages over the standard system. The points are replaced with trigger units with no moving parts, so once the timing is set there is no chance of it dropping out of adjustment through wear, unlike with the Lucas points. The wear-prone mechanical advance and retard mechanism is replaced with an electronically mapped advance curve, linked to the engine revs. The downsides of electronic ignition are minor – you cannot time each side of the engine individually and your battery needs to be properly charged for the system to work. Advantages are fit and forget,

The T100 makes a good mount for riding today. Here is a nice T100SS spotted at the Fleet Lions run in 2007.

accurate timing if set up correctly and sometimes easier starting. In addition, if you add up the cost of new coils, advance retard unit, points and condensers, then the cost of putting electronic ignition during a restoration is pretty much the same as putting decent-quality new parts on the bike. Conversion to points-in-side – the distributor is not the best mechanism for exact ignition timing. The combination of wear in the distributor and backlash in the drive gears makes exact ignition timing impossible to achieve.

Brakes
The Triumph twin leading shoe front brake from 1967 can be fitted to earlier bikes and gives a good increase in braking power. The brake was produced in three forms – the 1968-only 8in (20cm) unit, with the cable connecting to the brake at the back of the plate, the 1969–70 8in (20cm) unit with 'bell crank' cable operation, and the 1969–70 7in (18cm) unit, only ever fitted

with the 'bell crank' operation. However, a proper conversion is not necessarily straightforward. Firstly, while you can just fit the back plate into the 8in straight-spoke full-width hub, the braking area is not the full width of the hub. To gain the full benefit of the brake (either 7in or 8in) then the appropriate sized hub with the offset spoke flange should be used. The correct hubs are wider than the standard one, and, in order to fit the unit a set of 1969-onwards wider fork yokes is needed.

Jeff Cardew's T100SS

An old friend and neighbour of mine, Jeff Cardew bought his 1966 T100SS from the well known Triumph dealers Wests of Farnham in Surrey in 1976 when he was 18. Jeff ran the bike for some years and had many adventures and experiences with it that I've captured below. Probably the most striking note is the affection

The trouble with reminiscences is that the riders sometimes don't have pictures of their bike! This T100SS is just like Jeff Cardew's, however.

that he holds for the bike, despite the apparently endless list of problems he experienced with it. It was a bike that was worked hard, built in an era when you expected to have some problems and more maintenance running a British bike than with a Japanese one – perhaps customer expectations had been well managed by the British factories for some time!

Jeff suffered the indignity of running around on his Honda SS50 moped for two years while he was 16 and 17, before he was able to pass his motorcycle test and move onto a bigger bike. Jeff worked part time in one of the local motorcycle dealers, Wests in Farnham, Surrey, and found the green and cream T100SS in the shop at a price he could afford, using the SS50 as part exchange and selling his Scalextrix slot car set and other childhood toys to raise the balance. (As an aside, I bought my first real bike (well a BSA Bantam) from Wests for £20 as a 'spares or repairs' bike around the same time – when old British bikes were cheap as no one actually wanted them, in stark contrast to the classic market today!)

Jeff still looks back at his T100SS as the best bike he has ever owned, in terms of performance, character and fun. He recognizes it was not as fast or as reliable as the various Japanese bikes he ran (including a Honda CB500 four-cylinder and a Honda 750 four), and it needed a lot more maintenance, but he used it day in day out to commute in all weathers between his home in Odiham, Hampshire and Guildford Technical College in Surrey, where he was studying engineering, a round distance of about 18 miles (30km). The combination of performance and versatility was especially valued, none more so than when he went out in adverse weather conditions and used the bike as a trail bike. The bike was so dependable that Jeff used to really enjoy going out in the winter when it had snowed, as the handling was really well suited to the adverse conditions:

> I would seek out county lanes, you know, back lanes, with deep snow and with a friend with a trail bike we used to have great fun – and the Triumph was great fun, obviously not as good as the trail bike, but it was

just such a versatile bike. It was not too heavy, had tyres with tread on (in stark contrast to today's bikes) and could get up really steep hills in the snow. I'd just plonk it into second or third gear and chug up a hill slowly – it really was excellent. I have to wonder if we've lost a little bit with bikes now, they are too heavy and sophisticated and powerful. It was lovely.

The good times flowed for Jeff on the T100SS. He vividly remembers one incident concerning a humpback bridge, a mate on an A65 and a crowd of bemused tourists:

> I remember a friend of mine coming round to my house in Odiham on his BSA Lightning 650cc [in fact the rider was the my brother, Nick – and he was on the very same Lightning as featured in a previous book, *BSA Unit Construction Twins*], with another friend riding pillion We then all set off on our bikes, with me in the lead on the Triumph, and we decided to go towards Hartley Wintney. This involved crossing over the Basingstoke Canal via a humpback bridge. I remember we turned down the road, going towards the Water Witch public house, which, as it was summertime, had lots of people sitting outside in the beer garden. Everyone turned there head to look at these two noisy bikes, and then they looked away. Something snapped inside me – I don't know what it was, but I thought, "dammed cheek, looking away" – and the devil got hold of me and I dropped the bike down into third gear and opened her up. I went flying towards this bridge, that normally at 20–25mph (32–40km/h) on a bike you would be taking off – and I literally hit that thing at 70mph (112km/h). On the far side of the bridge the road dropped away and kept on dropping. I remember that I was so high that I was looking down at people's heads – not that they were slightly below me – I was way above them! The front wheel must have been 6ft, 8ft high (2m) – I absolutely flew. What was crazier was my friend slowed down to 65mph (104km/h) and also took off! I recently compared notes, thinking time must have exaggerated the memory, but he remembers it exactly as I did – we really flew. Both bikes just landed without a wobble or bottoming out the suspension or any damage, and I wonder how many of today's bikes could do that.

Tiger 100 500 c.c.

A truly great '500' – light in weight and easily handled by the experienced rider – the Tiger 100 is produced especially for the sports motorcyclist.

Progressively improved year by year to meet all the demands for higher performances from sports enthusiasts in the mediumweight range, this machine has gone from success to success in production motorcycle racing and has consistently proven its worth by annual gold medal honours in the International Six Days' Trial.

The new cylinder type Ignition Switch. Warning light fitted in headlamp.

The brochure shot of the 1966 T100SS shows what Jeff's bike looked like – when Jeff bought it the bike was pretty standard despite being ten years old.

It was not just jumping that the bike was good at – wheelies also featured in Jeff's repertoire. On a visit from his technical college to the Dennis Trucks factory outside Guildford one day he was carrying a fellow pupil on the pillion. Arriving at the Dennis factory, he had to go up a steep ramp to get to the car park. As he got to the ramp, Jeff opened her up and the bike lifted her front wheel and wheelied up the ramp and along the length of the factory car park. Unfortunately a security guard saw this and reported it as, 'some joker wheeling his bike in the car park', resulting in a reprimand to the whole class!

Jeff had the bike for around two years, and he rode it pretty hard: his throttle had two positions – off or full on!

Problems: well, in the words of Frank Sinatra, 'he had a few'; in fact, more than a few! In general Jeff found the bike quite maintenance intensive. Every other weekend he would have to redo the valve clearances and adjust the points, and he also found himself having to replace the tappet covers regularly as the threads and the slots in them got progressively looser! However, and Jeff was very proud of this, his T100SS did not leak oil – as he put it, 'one of the very few British bikes in use at that time that did not leak!'. His secret was not to use the standard 'cornflake packet' gasket on the casing, but to use orange silicon sealant. He would put a bead of gasket goo on the two mating surfaces and then leave it for an hour or so until the bead was tacky. Then he would put the casing back on loosely, with the two beads of silicone sealant just touching, and then leave it for another hour. Then he would tighten it all up, and was guaranteed that there would be no leaks. The downside of this method would be the excess sealant that was inside the cases – Jeff could trim off the outside, but there was still some inside – but it did not seem to have any adverse effects on the engine.

The first big mechanical problem Jeff had was unusual – the crank broke:

> I had not had the bike very long, and the crank cracked across one of the big end journals; I say it cracked, but actually it fractured all the way across the journal so the crank was in two halves. Luckily it fractured in such a way that the crankshaft wasn't actually able to flail, so it stayed together, but the whole engine just started to vibrate like crazy. It happened at the stage where I wasn't quite so brave about diving into engines myself, so I took it to Bert Gaymer, who ran a small shop in the backwoods of Farnham. [Bert was an ex-Meriden man, ex-ISDT rider who knew Triumphs inside out – now sadly passed away.] The news came back that the crankshaft was in two pieces – but he just put a new crankshaft in and the engine was fine. I think I was really lucky with that, as if the crankshaft had failed it would have just torn the engine apart. The trials and tribulations of Triumph ownership!

Another later problem that Jeff had with the bike was oil scavenging. Riding home to Odiham one evening along the 'Hogs Back', part of the A31 between Odiham and Guildford that runs along the top of a ridge giving spectacular views, he slowly began to realize that there was a problem:

> It was the winter, and I suddenly realized that one of my legs was feeling very warm, just below the knee. I didn't think too much about it at first but then I started wondering how come that leg was feeling warmer than the other? It got quite hot after a while, and I didn't pay too much attention to it, just thinking it was a bit strange. When I finally came to a corner and took it, it was 'wayyyyy-hoo' as the bike went quite wild – it went really wide and felt really unstable. I finally looked down, and my leg was completely

black, and there was hot oil bubbling out of the engine, making a heck of a mess! I stopped and had a look at this but didn't know what was happening – I just couldn't figure it out. So I continued my journey home to Odiham – but going a lot slower!

Further investigation revealed that the oil pump was not scavenging the oil out of sump, so the oil being pumped into the engine was finding all sorts of new ways to make its way out again, with very little getting back to the inside of the oil tank! Jeff can't remember now what exactly had gone wrong with the pump, but recalls it was easy to fix. It was probably one of the ball valves in the plunger oil pump not seating properly. Jeff is an advocate for the use of rotary oil pumps from an engineering viewpoint, and does not understand why Triumph struck with the plunger type for so long – although he recognizes that Triumph was running to a tight budget, and that many of the Triumph engineers were not keeping up with the times and new developments – and of course the plunger pump did work, was cheap to make and easy to drive off the camshaft, with no expensive helical drive gears to machine!

No story of a British bike is complete without an obscure electrical fault, and Jeff's tale of electrical woes really takes the biscuit. While the electrics were pretty good on the whole (vibration-induced damage not withstanding) the cause of one problem remains a mystery to Jeff:

> One of the coils went wrong, so I replaced it with one which I thought would do the job, but unfortunately it didn't. Somehow it made the cylinder run too hot, and that cylinder kept on seizing. It would seize, I had to quickly pull in the clutch and just coast for a short distance, and then it would be all right again. So what I would do was every few minutes was turn the ignition off, open the throttle wide and cool the engine down a bit with nice cold fuel! Then turn the ignition on and bang! as the unburnt fuel exploded in the exhaust – but the bike would keep going. I resolved the problem by getting the proper coil, but I still don't understand to this day why the wrong coil could make such a difference – it's weird.

Jeff was also less than complimentary about the method used to fix the fuel tank – the front bolt fixings were forever breaking free, and so he usually had a bid of a wobbly tank! Jeff eventually rubber mounted the fuel tank, and did voice some concerns over the tank-top parcel grid and its potential for emasculating a rider in a head-on collision!

Despite the dubious oil pump design, the bike was fundamentally reliable and served Jeff well. He is not blind to the bikes deficiencies, however, and could identify some improvements that he would make if he owned one today. Firstly he would replace the front forks with ones that were not as coarse and did not 'top out' as easily as the Triumph's did, and to get a bit more travel and a less harsh action. He also thought that rubber mounting the engine would be a good idea, both for extra comfort and to protect the electrics. On his bike, Jeff rubber mounted all the lights to give the bulbs a chance. Electronic ignition would be a must to remove the need to reset the points!

To quote Jeff: 'it was a fantastic bike!' What more can one say?

Rowena Hoseason's T100C

Rowena Hoseason is the joint editor and publisher, with Frank Westworth, of *RealClassic* magazine (see www.realclassic.co.uk), a classic bike magazine (and website) that was first published in the UK in 2004. However, Rowena has been involved in classic bikes for a good few years, and was a valued contributor to Classic Bike Guide for several years before setting up RealClassic with Frank. So she knows a thing of two about classics and shows some very good taste in possessing a 1971 Triumph T100C Trophy – and some possibly dubious taste by owning a Douglas Dragonfly 350cc twin, but that is another story! The 1971 T100C Trophy was the 'offroad' brother to the road-oriented Daytona, and the two bikes made up the sum total of the 'C' Series range that year. The 'C' Series bikes escaped the infamous Umberslade hall oil-carrying frame, forks and conical hubs, but did get some of the other features introduced that year – including indicators, the pressed tin 'gargoyle' rear light and abbreviated rear mudguard.

Rowena Hoseason's T100C is the bike that she would most like to keep. Here the drive side shows off the high-level exhaust.

Rowena's T100C is the most willing, easy-going old bike she's ever ridden. These are the exhaust pipes.

Rowena had had her T100C for some two years at the time of writing, and is still an enthusiastic owner. She had bought it because of the style that the bike oozed. The look of the bike, with its big wide handlebars and high level exhaust pipes, combined with its overall simplicity of the bike made a combination that she found impossible to resist – that and fact that it was less than half the price of a 650cc Trophy clinched the deal. The bike has 22,000 miles (35,000km) on the clock, and its condition and history suggest that the mileage is correct. Rowena knows the bike has done 10,000 of these miles (16,000km) in the last decade, so the bike is nicely run in. Mind you, there is the old adage that Triumphs run best when they are nicely run in, and that the 'nicely run-in stage' is not long before the 'a bit too loose and needs a rebuild soon' stage!

So, having owned the bike for some two years, Rowena has formed some firm opinions on what the bike is like. Probably most telling is the fact that she finds it 'the most willing, most easy-going old bike I've ever ridden'.

This is a real testament to the overall 'rightness' of the T100 design – Rowena's is a late model, and by then Triumph had managed to iron out virtually all of the major and minor problems that existed. The bike starts first or second kick – and it does not matter if the battery is flat – and it never needs any choke. The bike's state is just as Rowena likes it – good 'oily rag' state, not perfect, but with no major cosmetic problems, and in good mechanical condition. So Rowena is not afraid to take it out in the rain, and does not need to spend hours polishing it after a ride, giving her more time to ride it!

Rowena uses the bike for local rides, and it thrives on B and A roads where it is happy to cruise at 50–55mph (80–88km/h). At those speeds the bike bounds along and has lots in reserve so it can easily overtake anything it comes across. Any faster, and the bike gets a bit harsh and vibration starts to set in. At higher speeds, the bike's torque curve has peaked, and the engine is just giving more and more coarse high-rev power, which is not very pleasant. Rowena does not like to push an old bike beyond its comfort zone – and rightly so. If she wants to go faster, she takes a bigger bike! She also finds that above about 60mph (96km/h) the brakes become a bit marginal. The bike has the standard 7in (18cm) twin leading shoe brake, rather than the 8in (20cm) unit fitted to the Daytona. While this brake is good for a 250cc single, it starts getting flaky on a twin of twice the capacity.

Rowena lists the best things about the bike as 'manic muddy-lane meandering, the rorty exhaust note, its appearance and the fact it has never left me stranded by the side of the road (famous last words….)'. Her final comment is that the bike is 'a perfect example of how a model can be almost completely "right" just at the end of its development cycle. The Triumph 500cc twin – perfected near as dammit!'

So, all in all a pretty positive verdict from Rowena on the bike. But how does it stand up to its replacement in Triumph's 1970s range? Rowena's experiences in the old bike world have exposed her to all sorts of classic machinery, and importantly to several examples of the replacement for the T100C, the TR5T Adventurer/Trophy Trail with the BSA-derived oil-carrying frame. In comparing her T100C to the TR5T, she came up with the interesting observation that the T100C is a lot less 'stressy' than the TR5T, and is

Rowena Hoseasan's 1971 T100C.

a much nicer bike to ride both on- and offroad – not something that came up in the contemporary road tests, which tended to see the TR5T as the best thing since sliced bread!

Niggles? Rowena has very few. As mentioned above, the bike is just a bit harsh and vibratory at sustained high speeds, and she can't reach the 1971 indicator switch and keep her hand on the twist grip. While the first is a consequence of the bike's design and a consideration if you are buying one, the second is really part of the bike's character, and easily overcome if really necessary:

Rowena just does without her indicators! Overall, these are pretty minor faults that are more than made up for by the rest of the package. Her final gripe was that she was forever having to explain to people what the bike was – most spectators see the Triumph badge and assume it's a Bonneville: 'B' Series snobbery coming through!

Finally, when asked about her best ride on the Trophy, Rowena replied, 'Every ride, in fact, it's a grin-a-minute machine.' She went on to say: 'It'll probably be one of the bikes which stays in the shed for a very long time.' I could not have put it better!

The timing side of Rowena's T100C shows its 7in (18cm) TLS front brake.

Chris Goodburn's T100P

Chris Goodman bought his 1967 T100P in 2003, and had owned it for four years at the time of writing. It is a T100P model so was originally a police machine. Chris believes that the bike was exported to Rhodesia and used by the Rhodesian police, coming back into the country in the late 1990s. While Chris had ridden Matchless bikes in his youth and has his father's Matchless 350cc heavyweight single in his shed ready for restoration, he really wanted to try out the bike he had lusted after as a youth – and that bike was a Triumph unit twin. He had fancied both the 500cc Daytonas and Tigers and the 650cc Bonneville, but had never tried them. So when he decided to get a bike to keep him going while he restored the Matchless it had to be a unit Triumph. He decided to go for a 'C' Series 500cc rather than a 'B' Series 650cc for two reasons: the cost of a good 650cc bike was a lot more than a good 500cc, and he knew of a decent recently restored T100P that a friend owned.

Chris took two years to persuade his mate to sell the T100P to him. He was reluctant to let it go, but Chris eventually wore him down. As is common with T100Ps, this one has been restored to civilian specification. There are still some clues to the bike's origin – under the seat the battery carrier is larger than the civilian standard, and was designed to carry two batteries, and the tool carrier is a neat vertical box slotted in behind the battery carrier. Otherwise it's impossible to detect the bike's institutional past, apart from the 'T100P' prefix on the frame and engine – incidentally Chris's bike has matching frame and engine numbers, which is unusual for police machines.

The bike was equipped with a Boyer electronic ignition kit when Chris bought it, and while he has checked the ignition timing he has never had to alter it: it was spot on when he bought the bike, and has never shifted, a good advert for the system. It is also a good first or second kick starter from cold, although it can need three or four kicks when hot.

Chris uses the bike for riding about the area and also enters it into a number of charity shows

throughout the year – when he is not too busy helping to run them! The things he finds best about the bike are many, but probably the one that stands out is the way the bike rides. Chris was bought up riding big singles, AJSs and Matchlesses and with their low power but massive torque which you could just pootle along, keeping the bike in top gear, and letting the torque pull you out of corners with out having to use the gearbox. So the 'buzzy' nature of the Triumph is very appealing. He relishes the way the bike responds to revs and really enjoys taking it up and down the gearbox to get the best out of it. One of his favourite runs is a 30–40-mile (48–64km) round trip through the Hampshire and Surrey countryside, from Fleet out the Hindhead and back, taking in all the lovely back roads where the Triumph's lively nature can be exploited to the full. As he says, the hostelries are very nice along the

The under-seat layout of Chris Goodburn's T100P. Note the wide battery tray intended for twin 6v batteries, and the neat carrier for the tool roll behind the battery tray.

Police Bikes – The T100P

Triumph had a long history of providing bikes to both British and overseas police forces, and the 'C' Series twins were no exception. While lacking the outright performance of the 'B' Series 650cc twins, many police forces in the UK bought them. By the mid-1960s Triumph had a standard T100P model in the range, which was based on the T100S. Changes to the police bikes were relatively few, but making provision for radio kit and other police equipment meant that Triumph issued yearly supplements to the standard T100S parts manual to document the changes to standard specification. A study of some of these supplements reveals how Triumph made a number of minor tweaks and changes to the standard civilian bike specification to cater for this market.

Looking at the 1970 police specification and comparing it to the standard T100, the following significant changes are apparent. The engine was slightly detuned, by fitting pistons giving a compression ratio of 7.5:1 rather than the standard 9:1. Overall gearing was raised with a nineteen-tooth gearbox sprocket rather

than the standard eighteen-tooth item, and a single seat was fitted. New rear shock absorbers and a certified speedometer were fitted, along with a special fuel tank with provision to carry a radio in a recess in its top. The battery carrier was modified – presumably to carry two batteries, twin Lucas MLZ9Es being specified. Two Lucas 9H horns were fitted, along with a new alternator stator to handle the additional electrical load. A new rear mudguard and assorted brackets and lifting handle were also specified.

Reproduced opposite is the full set of changes made to the specification of the 1970 T100SS to turn it into a police bike. This table is a copy of the Triumph supplement to parts book Number 11, covering the 1970 'C' range twins. The list gives details of both replacement parts for the police models (identified in the table by the page and item number from 1970 Triumph 'C' Series Replacement Parts Catalogue No. 11), and new parts (so no page or item number) that supplement the standard machine specification.

Chris Goodburn's T100P was an ex-police bike, as evidenced by the 'T100P' prefix in the engine and frame numbers. Its fate – to be converted into 'civilian' trim – is typical of most ex-institutional bikes.

1970 Police Specification Parts List

Parts Catalogue Page	Parts Catalogue Item No.	Part No.	Description	Quantity
11	11	E7603	Piston assby. 7.5:1	1
32	1	T1476/19	Gearbox sprocket 19T	1
39	9	640/548/32	Suspension unit	2
53	n/a	F5733	Hinge bracket (single seat)	1
57	5	F8109	Battery carrier	1
		F7047	Battery carrier lining	1
		F7045	Battery separators	4
		F8110	Battery clip	1
		F5181	Rubber pad	1
		F8111	Rear battery carrier strap	1
		F5248	Rubber washer	1
		F5247	Spigot rubber	1
		S657	Rear bolt	1
		F4299	Washer bolt	1
		S25–1	Washer bolt	1
67	6	14-0301	Nut	1
		F7582	Support strap – horn relay	1
67	17	F4771	Bolt – horn relay to bracket	3
53	1	F11273	Police tank with pommels	1
		F9761	Radio tank	1
		F4645	Rubber moulding	1
		E2962	Stud – horn mounting	2
		W1691	Nut	2
53	34	F4893	Seat buffer (std. 2)	3
53	30	F8105	Single seat	1
53	37	F8107	Rear hinge	1
		S575	Starlock washer	1
53	39	DS57	Seat bolt	4
53	38	S26–2	Washer bolt	4
37	13	F7694	Centre stand	1
71	4	H2105	Bracket for speedo	1
71	1	SC5301/38	Speedometer mph	1
		SC5301/38	Uncertified chrono speedo mph	1
71	1	SC5301/37	Speedometer km/h	1
51	7	F11616	Rear mudguard	1
51	8	F7028	Bridge (mudguard)	1
51	5	F5030	Bracket, bottom front	1
		14-0126	Bolt, silencer to bracket	2
35	13	14-0303	Nut	2
57	1	MLZ9E	Battery	2
		54068152	Lucas 9H horn	1
		54068154	Lucas 9H horn	1
		33188	Horn relay	1
		F10018	Front bracket	1
		F6322	Rear bracket	1
		S2003	Stud – front engine plates to frame	1
33	4	D481	Rear chain (103 links)	1
51	9	F7860	Lifting handle	1
		E11339	Alternator	1
11	17	E11279	Nut, engine sprocket	1
33	22	E11344	Outer primary cover	1
33	26	E11278	Ignition pointer	1

As can be seen from the list there are a fair number of replacement or new parts, but not so many as to make it difficult to convert a police specification T100P back to 'civilian' trim.

Chris keeps his bike clean. Note the doubled-up clutch cable – an old trick where, in case of breakage, the new cable is ready to slot into place.

stretch and on a sunny summers evening there are few things that come close.

Chris has been fettling the bike since he bought it. The latest project has been to add a rev counter to give the handlebar layout a more balanced look and of course to let Chris know what the engine revs are, as he feels he is getting a bit enthusiastic in exploiting the bike's performance. Fitting a rev counter is straightforward, but involved sourcing both the instrument and a new dual instrument mounting panel on the fork top yoke, and also getting hold of the right drive box that fits onto the crankcases. The drive boxes are screwed to the crankcases and take their drive from the end of the exhaust cams. Chris's bike is an early model and has a 'standard' thread into the

cases to fix the drive box in place – this fitting was replaced in later models with a left-hand thread to counter the fixing screw's propensity to undo itself due to vibration   – so Chris has been advised to use 'locktight' to firmly fix the screw in place or be plagued with a self dissembling drive!

The main downside for Chris is the size of the bike, which is a bit small for him, especially when compared with a T120 Bonneville. He finds it a bit cramped, but puts some of it down to his age, and the fact that the old body can't quite accommodate what it could in his youth – as he says the bones creak and don't mould to the riding position! In addition, he finds it a pain to pull the bike up onto the main stand – not too much of a problem as the bike has a side stand which works well. Good points about the bike abound. It has 12v electrics and the lights are excellent – much better than the bikes Chris rode in his youth – making it easy to ride in the dark. In addition, he has had no electrical problems, apart from one blown main fuse (ironically suffered when I was giving the bike a test ride after setting up the carburettor for Chris) the cause of which Chris and I have been unable to identify. However, a classic British bike has to have at least one obscure electrical fault otherwise it is not a real classic! Ideas for the future include fitting a carrier on the back, which Chris feels will also help with pulling the bike up onto its centre stand. As Chris says – there's nothing about the bike he doesn't like, just a couple of niggles. There are still things he wants to do to it, but he is really happy and pleased with the bike and looks forward to putting many more miles on it in the future.

Simon Smith's Daytona T100R

Simon Smith was a fellow pupil of mine at Yateley Comprehensive School in the 1970s. As we approached the age that we were allowed to ride real motorcycles (17), the school was split between those who wanted the performance and reliability of the Japanese, and those who were firmly wedded to the rapidly declining British industry. Simon started his motorcycling on a

The only picture of Simon Smith's 1974 model but 1976-registered Daytona. Despite being the great Meriden disintegration machine, Simon enjoyed a good few miles on it!

Honda CB125 – a nippy single that easily out-performed the Tiger Cub of Steve Brewer, one of the main proponents of the British camp! When Simon passed his test, and wanted a bigger bike, one of the considerations was the cost of insurance. The popular 750cc class of bike was unaffordable, so he decided to limit himself to a maximum of 500cc.

The bike of choice was the newly introduced Honda 400/4, and one of the pupils in the next year up (Ian 'Jack' Hargreaves) had just such a bike. It lived up to Honda's reputation for reliability, buried the myth that all Japanese bikes did not handle and was remarkably quick. This was 1976, and the Meriden sit-in was in full flow, but there were some 1974 model Triumph Daytonas released from the factory and in the dealers' showrooms. And another pupil at Yateley, Chris Marr, bought one. It was another quick bike for its size, and in a burn-off with Jack's 400/4 if was

demonstrably faster. This led to Simon deciding to go for a Daytona, along with the facts that the bigger bike was £100 less than the Honda and made a much better noise! Simon bought his Daytona from the local Triumph dealer, Ken Heanes in Fleet. Ken was a famous Triumph works rider, competing in many ISDTs. The Daytona was in fact a US model T100R, in blue and white, with the twin leading shoe front brake – not as modern as the disc on the Honda, but it did work in the wet!

The handling of the Daytona was, to quote Simon, 'brilliant'. He still remembers riding it two up down the 'Fleet Bends' between Yateley and Fleet, with another school friend, Peter Isted, on the back. The bike could be leant over until the pillion's feet were scraping on the road, and in this case the bike was cornering so hard that the nails in the soles of Pete's boots were pushed up into his feet!

This is a brochure shot of Simon's 1974 Daytona, showing what it looked like before it started to disassemble itself!

Simon's best-remembered moment was out-running a police van coming back from the Swan Inn (now sadly a housing estate) in Hartley Wintney one night on his way home. The route he took back to Blackwater was along the A30 – fairly straight and long, especially past Blackbushe Airfield. Simon was two up at the time, reckons he touched 105mph (169km/h) along the road, and his pillion was asleep – and stayed asleep all the way home! The road holds some terror as well – Simon's worst moment on the bike was when the headlamp loosened off and swivelled down going past Blackbushe Airport – he couldn't see a thing until he managed to pull it back up again! The downside is encapsulated in Simon's description of the bike as the 'Great Meriden Disintegration Machine'! The bike did tend to disassemble itself, and there are probably still bits

of nearly new Daytona scattered throughout the roads of north Hampshire. This was especially true of the rocker covers, and Simon used to carry a couple around with him all the time as emergency replacements. The bike also had some other problems which were probably down to it sitting in Meriden for two years. With just 16 miles (26km) on the clock, it developed a massive oil leak. On taking it back to Ken Heanes's shop the head of Service said 'bring it in next week' – luckily Ken Heanes was there and he made the service department fix it there and then, but it was not a good start to ownership for Simon. After a year, Simon traded the bike in for a new Suzuki GS750 – a much more sophisticated and reliable bike and a quantum leap in performance. Simon still has fond memories of the bike, though, representing as it did his first 'big' bike.

6 Restoration

Firstly, a word about safety. This chapter describes the methods and techniques that I use to restore a bike. Anyone who embarks on such a product should be aware that there are dangers associated with working on old bikes. Old oil, petrol and other fluids used in old bikes can be toxic, there is a strong likelihood that there will be asbestos in the brake shoes and in the dust in the drums, and there is a constant risk of injury from sharp tools and bits of bike. Anyone who decides to restore their own bike should only do jobs that they are competent to do, and take all safety precautions that are needed.

Obvious as it seems, the first step to doing a restoration is to find a bike to restore. Deciding what bike to restore is a personal thing, and factors influencing your choice range from reliving the bikes of your youth to having an academic interest in a particular marque or model. I chose to restore a 'C' Series Triumph for several reasons. The bikes are an interesting contrast to the 650cc Triumph T120R I own, and were a successful range in their own right. Friends of mine have owned them – and still do – and liked them. Memories from my youth and recent research reveal that the bikes are quick, light and manoeuvrable. In contrast to many British bikes, these small Triumphs are revvers rather than sloggers, and have a different character to the larger twins – to use a doggy analogy, more of a springer spaniel than a Labrador.

As bought, the 1969 Trophy was a rolling chassis, with the engine separate, and no exhaust system. The front forks were complete, and had 'offroad' shrouds above the springs, showing this model probably never had lights fitted.

As bought, the bike was in need of a total restoration. But, importantly, all the tinware was present, including the stainless steel mudguards.

So the hunt was on, but which model to choose? As the model was in production from 1957 to 1974 there are plenty around, and the range presented me with tourers, sportsters and offroad models. The early touring models did not really appeal – while the bathtub styling is a Triumph icon, I do not particularly like large expanses of tinware. The roadster sports models always lived in the shadow of the larger twins, and were pretty common in the UK. I eventually decided that what a really wanted was one of the US models, with their high pipes and small fuel tanks. Finding one in the condition I wanted and at the price I wanted to pay was always going to be interesting. As I was going to carry out a full restoration condition was not too important, as long as the main parts (frame, forks, engine, wheels, fuel and oil tanks, and mudguards) were present. Spares availability for most of the ancillary items is generally good, many being shared with the larger 'B' Series twins, so anything missing should not present too big a challenge. As it was a Triumph, matching

engine and frame numbers would be a bonus.

So now having decided roughly what I wanted, it was time to set the chase in motion. EBay was one source that I have used in the past to source bikes, but I find now that even basket cases are commanding high prices – good for the seller, but not for a buyer. I put out feelers to local bike shops and various contacts in the classic bike world, and, when these failed to turn up anything started to hit the classic bike magazines. Basket cases rarely seem to appear in the classifieds, so I started to contact the dealers that advertise in the press. I had turned up my Triumph Bonneville and T25SS basket cases this way some years previously, and once again the method paid off. Yeoman's in the West Midlands had a T100C, late 1960s vintage with matching engine and frame numbers.

While it was not complete and had obviously been used as an offroader, it was mostly there, and the price was right. A 180-mile (290km) round trip up the M4 and M5 motorways with the trailer one Saturday morning resulted in the right amount of money changing hands, and a US-spec T100C rolling chassis, with the engine and a range of rusty, oily bits in the car's boot, heading back to my garage/workshop. Research into Roy Bacon's Triumph Twins and Triples indicated that as the bike had an engine/frame number in the H66nnn range, it was an early 1969 model.

Getting Started

Initial Assessment

When setting off on a restoration, it is important to do an initial assessment to see what is obviously present, and what is not! Before buying the bike, you will hopefully have assessed the spares situation so will know what is and is not available, and can make sure when you buy a wreck you that all the unobtainable parts are present. Luckily with the small unit Triumphs,

spares availability is good, and there are few parts that are really rare.

With the T100C all the main bits were there: frame, engine, front forks, fuel and oil tanks, wheels, and mudguards. What was also gratifying was that most of the under-seat steel pressings were present (oil tank mounting plates and battery carrier), and that the side panel was in reasonable condition, apart from two holes drilled in its lower half to carry two switches. Stainless steel mudguards were fitted, and while the rear one had some extra holes in it, front and rear were in usable condition. I do like stainless steel mudguards. Not only are they 'fit and forget', they look good and don't need to be painted, so good news all round.

The fuel tank was a very strange shade of green, and had some badly faded and bubbled gold 'scallops'. Basically the paintwork was not recoverable, and it was debatable if it was original. The tank should be Lincoln Green with a

Closer inspection showed that the battery carrier, oil tank and side panel were all present, but in need of refurbishment.

Specials

The Triumph engine being light, compact and easily tuned lent itself to being fitted into frames from other makes. One of the most famous frame makers, alongside Eric Cheney, was Rickman Brothers, with their Metisse (French for mongrel) frame. Built in top-quality tubing, the frame was adapted for both on- and offroad use, and was built in various sizes to accommodate engines from 125cc two-strokes up the awesome Kawasaki Z1 900cc unit!

The Rickman frame was usually supplied in kit form for the buyer to source a suitable engine and build the bike up. The kits were pretty comprehensive, and included ancillary items such as fuel and oil tanks and seat units. Forks could be supplied by Rickman, or could be taken from the donor bike. The Rickman chassis was very highly regarded at the time, and gave excellent handling and road holding.

Other specials builders used frames from existing bikes. The T100 unit was so light and compact that it could be persuaded into many frames originally designed for smaller engines. A popular frame for conversions in the 1960s was (and still is) the Greeves unit. This frame was unique in the British motorcycle world in that it had a distinctive cast alloy front member which included the headstock. Greeves were mainly engined using Villiers two-strokes, and range up to 350cc with the Villiers 4T twin. Luckily, the use of front engine mounting plates on the 'C' Series engine meant that it was short enough to fit in the Greeves frame.

The Tri-Greeves hybrid was quite popular, and can either be made up as a trail or a pure road bike. Either way, the frame performs well, and the unique Greeves rubber in torsion front forks ensure an excellent ride. Still on the subject of re-engining of two stroke machines, here is a relatively modern special, Fred Burbridge's Bultaco TSS-based racer. Pictured at the CRMC meeting at Cadwell Park in October 2004, the bike is engined with a Triumph 500cc engine.

The next bike in this section gives an idea of the versatility of the Triumph 'C' Series engine. Good on- and offroad, in racing, trials and scrambles it was also a popular power plant for grass-track racing. Illustrated is a Hagon-framed, T100A-engined bike from the 1960s. It just goes to show that you can't keep a Triumph engine down!

There are no limits to what some people will do to make a special. The bike illustrated below is simple identified as a Rod Coates Triumph, and is a 1000cc four-cylinder device – made by grafting a second unit 500cc engine in front of the first!

Looking at the engines you can see that the rear engine's cylinder head has been put on back to front to give clearance for the exhaust system, and that there are two Amal Monobloc carburettors, presumably each feeding one engine via special manifolds.

How the engines are linked together is unclear, especially as the front engine seems to have bee put in back to front. There is a large, home-made cover over the drive side (right-hand side) of the front engine, and it looks like there are contact breaker points present on both engines – albeit on opposite sides. All in all, this is a spectacular example of the special builder's work!

If the buyer wanted, the Rickman Metisse frame came as a kit for self assembly.

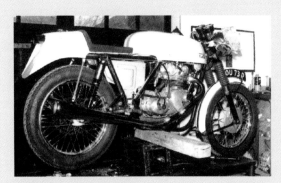

Building up a Rickman kit only needed a decent donor bike and a workshop.

This 5TA-engined Greeves-framed special was seen at the New Brighton road race in the summer of 1966.

The Bultaco TSS frame could take a Triumph engine. Fred Burbidge and his 500cc Triumph-engined special were pictured at the CRMC meet at Cadwell Park in 2004.

Grass track racing was not immune from the 'C' Series Triumph. This Hagon frame packs a T100A engine, and was pictured in 1960.

The Triumph-engined Coates special puts a whole new meaning on the term 'Triumph Twin' – or should that be Twin Triumph Twins with its two T100 engines?

Putting the two engines into one frame and getting them to fit must have caused some headaches for Ron Coates.

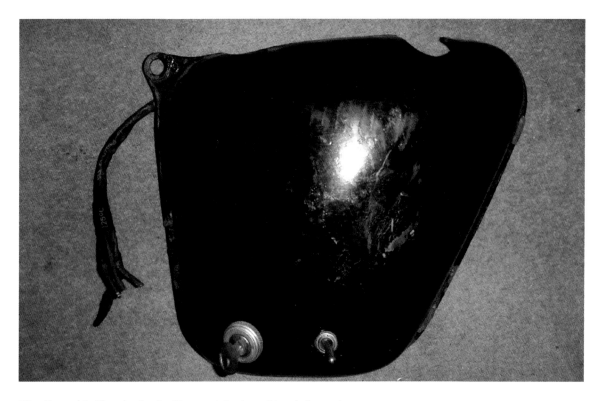

The side panel had been butchered, with two switches inserted into its lower edge.
These must have been inaccessible with the standard high-level exhaust.

central stripe in silver, and looked to have been (badly) resprayed at some stage. Inside the filler cap there was some evidence that the tank may have been from a 1970 model, with its rather lurid Jacaranda Purple finish. There were no tank fixing studs, bolts and rubbers and the circular reflector housings that sit at the base of the front of the tank were missing. However, it was not all bad news as the tank was apparently undented, had its knee grips, badges and fuel taps and even had the central chrome trim strip and fittings. The threads for the tank's front fixing studs in the 'towers' were in good condition. The side panel and oil tank were painted a rather vibrant shade of red rather than black, and the oil tank filler cap, drain plug and filter were also covered in the same red paint – even the edges of the sealing washers, indicating that the unit had been painted somewhat carelessly. While the oil tank had a couple of shallow dents, the lower part of the side

panel had collected two holes for the aftermarket ignition and light switches which would need to be welded up.

The electrics were virtually non-existent, with a very battered rectifier under the seat, no battery, wiring loom, Zener diode or lights. However, the horn was present – an original item still mounted under the fuel tank, along with the condenser pack, fitted by the horn. The pair of non-standard switches let into the side panel would have to go, and the resulting holes would need to be welded up, otherwise the panel was in good condition and was the correct version, with the tool roll carrier incorporated in it. The panel was simply bolted onto the frame at the front, when there should have been a plastic-headed knurled knob and a captive nut on the frame; these components are easy to get and are shared with the 650cc models. The seat base had a rust hole in it and while the cover was

OK, the plastic 'chrome' trim that goes around the base was cracked and corroded. The rear brake pedal was (surprisingly) unbent and still had its original stop and pivot bolted to the frame. There was no stoplight switch, and the chain guard was already off the bike.

The first interesting point with the bike was the front wheel. Initial research had suggested that a 1969 model T100C should have the 7in (18cm) twin leading shoe front brake, but this example had a 7in single leading shoe brake in the earlier hub. Further investigation showed that the T100C only got the TLS brake and flanged hub after engine/frame number XC07583 – prior to that the model had the 1968 SLS brake. The bits that needed attention were relatively few, and comprised the front forks top covers, which were devoid of the headlamp ears; the wheel rims and spokes, which were starting to corrode; tyres, which were both offroad types and very hard and worn; the paintwork, which was all old, non-standard and worn; and the footrests, which were heavily modified with reinforcing metal being welded on.

The engine had its head off and primary drive dismantled. The head needed some work – there were no valves or springs, and the pistons also had some quite heavy marks on their tops that were distinctly non-standard. The big ends and main bearing appeared to be in reasonable shape, and the engine could be turned over using a spanner on the crank pinion, but felt a bit stiff. The gearbox seemed to be fine, with no play on the main shaft and all gears present. The primary drive was dismantled and in a cardboard box, but most of the big bits were there. There was no alternator rotor or stator, but as I always replace both items with new equivalents on any of my rebuilds this was not a problem.

Stripping Down

Now that the initial assessment of the condition of the bike was completed, the strip-down could commence, making notes of any problems or missing parts. I tend to ignore the engine at this stage, treating it as a separate lump, and limiting any dismantling to whatever is needed to get it out of the way – as the engine was already out of the frame, there was nothing to do yet. Taking off all of the bits and pieces that make up the rolling chassis is relatively easy, but you need to check and note any problems, such as stripped threads, damaged tinware, missing brackets and so on. Luckily the T100C did not seem to be missing anything obvious, and inspection of the parts manual during the strip reinforced this view.

The forks had new head bearings, nicely packed with clean (red) grease, but the yokes

This 500cc twin with twin carburettors was pictured in 1960 – well before the advent of the Daytona.

needed painting, the chrome plating on the fork seal holders was gone, and the sliders needed paint. The fork stanchions looked to be in reasonable condition. I always replace the fork bushes as a matter of course, and would assess the stanchions' condition when the new bushes are installed, but I did not anticipate having to change them. The aforementioned fork top covers would need replacing. The fork top nuts all needed replacing as the chrome was bad and they all showed signs of previous butchery. If possible I usually source stainless steel items for these, along with stainless fork seal holders and new seals.

Planning

With the initial assessment and strip down complete, the planning can be started. You don't need to go into too much detail, just have a set of objectives that fit together. In this case (and in all the restorations I've done) I aim to get a rolling chassis complete before the engine. This gives me a target to achieve with reasonably quick results – always important. If you start a restoration by doing lots of the little jobs but have no chassis to fit them to, you will have no evidence of any progress other than refurbished parts scattered throughout the workshop, which can be dispiriting some months into the restoration. Hence my first aim is to get the frame blasted and painted, and the wheels rebuilt. Then, with the forks reconditioned the rolling chassis can be quickly put together. The engine can be checked over and renovated as necessary once the rolling chassis is complete, and then installed. The electrics will be the last job to do, although the lights and electrical fitting will be fixed onto the rolling chassis as and when it is convenient.

Wheels

Disassembly

While the frame was off being 'done' I got the wheels disassembled, cleaned up the hubs, checked the wheel bearings and then reassembled the wheels with new rims and spokes.

The wheels that came with the bike looked reasonable, but closer inspection showed that the chrome on both was just starting to lift on the OE Dunlop rims. This was a shame, as it would have been nice to reuse them – and of course cheaper. The spokes and nipples were showing signs of corrosion, the front hub was rusty on its outside finned edge and the rear hub also needed repainting. The rear wheel bearings were in good condition and reusable, but surprisingly the front bearings were badly worn. Maybe this indicates that the bike had spent time with its front wheel on and off the ground, and bashing into obstacles in cross country events!

Starting with the front wheel, the rim and spokes were removed by undoing the nipples using an open-ended ¼in AF spanner. On the front hub, the spokes are straight, so seized spokes can be a problem as it is difficult to grip the spokes without damaging the finish. I was not too concerned with protecting the spokes as I was planning to replace them anyway. While some of the spokes were stiff, holding them with pliers usually allowed the nipple to be unscrewed. Only one nipple had seized up, and this actually snapped the spoke. While the recommended way to dismantle a wheel is use bolt cutters to cut all the spokes and let the hub drop out, I prefer to dismantle wheels by hand. Cutting the hub out may be the only practical option with a badly rusted wheel, but there are a number of advantages in trying to dismantle the wheel first. Firstly, you end up with some or all of the spokes in one piece, making it easier to match up the replacements, and it also gives you emergency spares. You also get a feel for the spoke pattern, and in which order the wheel needs to be rebuilt. Once the rim was off, the hub could be refurbished. Stripping the bearings out of the front hub revealed that some work had been carried out on the wheel before, with the wrong grease retainer behind the brake side bearing, while on the other side of the hub the bearing retaining circlip was missing all together.

With the hub bare, it was ready to be cleaned up and painted. The rust on the perimeter of the hub was cleaned off using a rotary wire brush, as

*Rebuilding a wheel is fiddly but not too difficult. I use an old BSA C15 swinging
arm clamped in a workbench as a rebuilding jig. Alloy rims and stainless steel spokes
will give long service with minimum corrosion.*

was the inside. Remember to be extremely cau-
tious and wear appropriate protective gear when
working on any brake parts as asbestos dust may be
present and represents a major health risk. Once it
was cleaned up, and the new bearings were in place
the hub was painted using silver Finnigans
Smoothrite in aerosol cans – a paint I tend to use
a lot for this type of application, as it goes on evenly and smoothly, is hard wearing and has a finish
very close to the original. Also it is easy to spray a
hub – you just put the spindle back in and hold it
in a vice. Then if you spin the hub, you can spray
the outer edge of the hub quickly and evenly.

The rear wheel bearings were OK, but to
rebuild the wheel, the bolt-on brake drum
(which has a bolt-on sprocket) had to be removed
as it covered the ends of the drive side spokes.
This was easily done by undoing the eight nuts
and bolts that held it on to the hub. With the
brake drum off the hub, the ends of the drive-side
spokes were exposed and the rim could be

removed. As the spokes had a 90-degree turn at
the end there was no need to use pliers to hold
them, and they all came off easily. This left the hub
exposed, which only needed some touching up
with black paint.

Rebuilding
Rebuilding the wheels onto the refurbished hubs
was a relatively painless affair. I ordered new
flanged alloy rims and stainless steel spokes from
Central Wheel Co., and with the old spokes and
rims to hand it was easy to check that I had the
right-sized spokes, which spokes went where on
the wheel, and that the rims were correctly
punched. I discovered that the spokes for the
front wheel were the wrong length, and had to
return them to Central Wheel for a replacement
set – there had been a mix-up on the front hub
diameter.

I carried out the initial assembly of the
wheels flat on the ground, putting in one row of

spokes first, followed by the second row on the same side, making sure the second row fitted over the first for ease of assembly. Each spoke was only loosely fitted, giving plenty of flex for fitting the next row. With one side completed, the wheel was turned over and the other side laced up in the same way, resulting in a complete wheel that needed all the spokes tensioning up and the wheel truing. Applying a bit of lateral thinking on the wheel building front, I used a C15 swinging arm that I had left over from a previous restoration as a wheel building jig. Clamping it vertically in the trusty Black and Decker workmate, it supported the loosely built wheels perfectly, making it easy to true the wheel. By holding a pointer against the wheel rim and spinning the wheel is is easy to see where the wheel is out of true.

I initially tensioned all spokes up using a battery-powered hand drill with a torque setting, basically screwing the nipples until the drill started to ratchet on its lowest torque. This gave me a

wheel with equally tensioned spokes, that I could start to true up.

There are four things to get right when wheel building – ensure that the rim is at the correct offset to the hub, the rim edges are flat, the rim is concentric to the hub, and finally the rim is true side to side. To get the offset right, you move the rim relative to the hub by loosening one side of spokes, and tightening the other side, which pulls the rim over. If the rim is tilted in relation to the surface of the hub, tighten the spokes on the side it is high to pull it back down. If the rim is running up and down, then loosen the high side and tighten to low side spokes. Once the rim is running true and concentric to the hub, I take out any side-to-side wobble by loosening the spokes on one side, and tightening the spokes on the other side to pull that part of the rim into line. Once the wheels were trued and the spokes properly tightened, I checked the outside edge of the rim for any spokes protruding through the nipple. As this could result in a punctured inner

When a wheel has been rebuilt, make sure you grind down the ends of any spokes that protrude through the nipple on the inside of the rim. The end of the spoke could fret through the rim tape and inner tube, causing a puncture.

tube, they were ground down using a Dremmel-type mini tool. Then I could fit the tyres, which would mean that the wheels were ready to go on, and, probably more importantly, that the new rims would be protected from being scratched or knocked. I decided to use Dunlop K70s, which were standard fitment in the 1960s and are still available, albeit made in Japan and using modern rubber compounds giving reasonable wear and excellent wet and dry grip. New rim tapes and inner tubes were also used. It is a false economy using the tubes and tyres that come with a restoration project unless you know their history. Tyres, tubes and rim tapes deteriorate over time – the Dunlop Trials Universals that came with the T100 were rock hard, and showed signs of cracking in the sidewalls. The use of rim tapes is also important. While some people recommend using insulation tape, this not a good idea as it can trap moisture and promote rust in the spoke ends, nipples and inside of the rim, which in turn can lead to punctures.

I fitted the new tyres using talcum powder as a lubricant to keep use of levers to a minimum. I used to use washing-up liquid as a lubricant for tyres, but as it has a very high salt content it can wreak havoc with spokes, nipples and rims, causing rust that can lead to punctures. Talc is relatively benign, and is also dry so does not cause anywhere near as many problems, although it is worth getting non-perfumed talc if possible – my workshop did smell like a lady's boudoir for some weeks after fitting!

Frame and Rolling Chassis

Repainting
Most if not all of the Triumph's frame and fittings are painted black. The approach I take is to get the big bits professionally shot blasted and powder coated in gloss black. The smaller bits I clean up and paint myself. There were lots of small brackets and fittings on the frame which were originally painted black, such as mudguard brackets, engine plates, rear footrest hangers and the battery carrier assembly. All of these were suffering from corrosion and tatty paint. I removed the paint using a rotary wire brush in the power drill, and, once stripped back to bare metal are either brush or spray painted with black Finnigans Smoothrite enamel. This paint gives a decent smooth gloss finish even when applied directly to bare metal, is long-lasting and kills any existing rust. It is easy to apply and only has two minor disadvantages: it takes some time to dry completely, and you must put the second coat on within about six hours otherwise the two coats will react and bubble.

Meanwhile the frame, oil tank, side panels and other larger pieces were away at the blaster's to get all the old paint off, and then at powder coater's. A good powder coater will blank off any threads and other holes (such as the head lug) where you do not want the paint to go – if in doubt tell the powder coater what you want blanked off or do it yourself! My three main parts – the main frame loop, the rear loop and the swinging arm – came back from the powder coaters looking superb, ready to be reassembled.

Reassembly
To facilitate the assembly, and to save my back, I put the main frame loop on the trusty Black and Decker workmate and fastened it on with large cable ties. This raised the frame up to a sensible working height, making the subsequent assembly of the rolling chassis easier.

The rear swinging arm is supported on two bushes in the frame, and these need to be line reamed to fit the swinging arm pin. I used an adjustable reamer, and was careful to ensure that the bushes were reamed in line. The swinging arm should be fitted before the rear sub-frame, as the sub-frame carries two plates that support the end of the swinging arm pivot – a major factor in improving the bike's handling. The rear sub-frame bolts onto the main frame with a tubular bush at the top and two large bolts on each side at its base.

With the frame bolted back together the minor components could be put back on to the frame, using new bolts and rubber bushes where needed.

*The 1969 bike had the third type of frame used on the T100, with the thick top rail.
Powder coating gives a good tough finish.*

*The top rail and steering head make for
a rigid assembly. Note the steering lock
hole on the flange on the top of the
steering head, and the way the flange
extends around the steering head to
prevent the lock from being engaged
accidentally.*

It is important to thoroughly clean out the oil tank before starting the cleaning and painting process, to ensure that all of the blasting residue is purged. A lot of people recommend that oil tanks are not blast cleaned, and I can sympathize with this view. However, if you do decide to have an oil tank blasted, then you should wash it out properly before sending it to the blaster's, as the sticky sludge left in the tank is excellent at retaining blasting grit. Gunk or an equivalent degreaser/cleaner is the best thing to clean it out with. The blaster will appreciate having a clean tank to play with, and you should get back a tank that is easy to get all the grit out of. Washing it through with water a lot of times should clear out the grit; thorough drying out (the airing cupboard springs to mind) and a final swish round with oil should prevent any internal rust from forming.

The side panel and oil tank presented me with a bit of a problem. Both had some small dents in them, and the side panel had had the holes in it braised, which also needed some finishing. My local sprayers all seemed reluctant to take on the job of spraying them gloss black, and quoted what seemed to my mind unreasonable prices. They were probably too big to be painted using Smoothrite, so I decided to try spraying them myself with aerosol paint. While I have had success using Smoothrite to paint smaller items, I've never had much success with spraying larger items, so had to read up on the subject before attempting it. Four things stood out in the 'how to spray' guides – get a good, smooth base, only put on a small amount of top coat at one time, spray in a clean environment and take your time, don't rush. Safety was another important aspect. Aerosol paints will give safety information on the can, and anyone using them is advised to heed these instructions, especially avoiding inhaling the fumes.

I started off by rubbing down the previously sandblasted side panel and then sprayed it with a primer filler. I decided to start with the side panel as it only had a few small dents and creases in it, while the oil tank had quite a large dent. I filled the dents with plastic filler, rubbed them down, and then gave the panel about six thin coats of primer filler, allowing plenty of time for each coat to dry. Each coat comprised one layer of paint sprayed from side to side and one sprayed from top to bottom, giving an even but thin coat. I then set about rubbing down the paint on the cover with 800 grade wet and dry paper, used wet. This exposed many more small blemishes and these were filled with cellulose filler, and the panel resprayed with primer filler again, with another six or so coats put on. Again the primer was rubbed down and inspected, and again any blemishes were filled and rubbed back. Plenty of time (days) were left between spraying and rubbing down to allow time for the paint to harden. If, as I did, you start rubbing down before the paint is dry you risk marking the paint – I had a couple of palm prints impressed into the panel when rubbing it down, which is a good way of identifying the panel as yours but does nothing for the end result!

Once the panel was primed, filled and rubbed back (after about four of the above cycles!) it was time to put on the top coat. This I did very slowly, putting about two to three coats on each evening over two to three days. Then it was time to rub back to make sure the base coat was level – and invariably on the first rubdown the high spots were revealed. I rubbed the top coat down with 1200 wet and dry, used cellulose putty to fill any significant blemishes, and then sprayed the complete panel again. It was surprising how many blemishes that I had not noticed while priming appeared at this stage, but luckily they were relatively shallow so could be filled with the putty. Again the spray and rubdown cycle was followed about four times, putting more and more paint on. The final finish was achieved by rubbing down with 1500 grade wet and dry paper, followed by a fine cutting paste. This rather lengthy process resulted in a pretty good, deep shine, and I repeated the process on the oil tank.

The side panel needed two new rubber bushes and a new fixing knob and screw before it could be refitted. The oil tank also needed new top and bottom rubber bushes and top mounting pins to make a neat and tidy job of mounting it onto the frame. A new filler cap was also needed as the chrome on the original one had long since disappeared. The drain plug and internal gauze filter had the red paint removed from them and were cleaned up and refitted with new sealing washers.

The final part that needed fitting under the seat was the battery carrier. The carrier assembly that came with the bike was in good condition – though this is a part that often suffers from leaking battery acid. The assembly is made up of two crosspieces and the carrier, which slots onto the crosspieces and is located by a couple of studs and nuts. A motley assortment of rubber bushes, studs and nuts enables the crosspieces to be connected to the frame.

I disassembled the assembly, cleaned the carrier and crosspieces and painted them using Smoothrite. One end of each crosspiece mounts on a lug on the drive side of the frame using rubber bushes, and the other end bolts onto the oil tank fixing studs, which are rubber mounted through to the frame. Once positioned, the battery carrier can be lowered onto the crosspieces and secured in position using the two nuts on the studs – one of which doubles up as a locating knob for the battery strap. The rubber bushes can be tricky to position if used dry, but using proprietary rubber lubricant makes the job easy. I would also recommend new bushes – they are cheap and easy to obtain, and the old ones will have hardened with age and are likely to look pretty ragged. With the carrier fixed in position, a new rubber mat in place for the battery, and a new battery strap and anchoring plate in place, the under-seat area was complete.

I decided to reuse the seat, but to look out for a new chrome trim strip, and to repair the hole in the seat base with glass-fibre. The only other work needed to the seat was to put a seat check wire. Interestingly Rockerbox did not stock

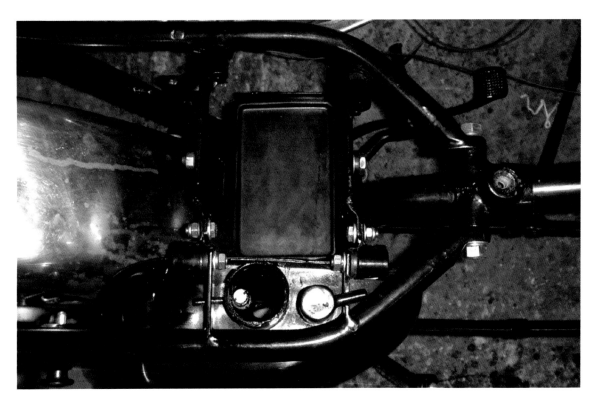

The under-seat layout coming together – the oil tank and battery carrier are rubber mounted onto fixings on the frame.

them, as they claimed they always broke. So I made one up by silver soldering (as its name suggests, silver solder contains a good proportion of silver, and is a lot stronger than standard solder) a couple of electrical ring terminals onto a suitable length of Bowden cable from an old throttle cable. Screwed and bolted into place, it prevented the seat from hitting the newly painted side panel when it was opened. A couple of good pushes on the open seat did not break it, so it seems to be strong enough. However, as the restoration progressed, it became obvious that the seat foam was disintegrating – the bits of bike under the seat were getting covered in a fine brown dust, despite the holes in the seat base being filled. So I splashed out on a new seat, courtesy of Rockerbox.

In the original bike the small plate-type rectifier was attached to a lug on the back of the battery carrier, but as I'm using the Sparx combined regulator/rectifier unit I don't need one on the bike. The Sparx electronic ignition unit was fitted into the tool carrier in the right hand side panel. Bolted in place, it was secure, and as the side panel is rubber mounted, it will hopefully not get too much vibration. The output wires from the unit terminate in a plug that connects into the new loom, so the panel can still be removed, although the close proximity of the upswept exhaust makes it a major fiddle to get it clear without damaging the paint or my hands on hot exhaust pipes!

The front footrests presented me with some challenges. The model should have folding footrests for offroad use, but the units that came with the bike had been heavily modified. There was a serrated tube welded onto the footrest itself, and a bracing bracket connecting the footrest to the mounting hanger. This meant that the footrests were pretty strong but no longer folded.

My quest for new folding footrests was semi-successful – I found a set of new old-stock footrest hangers at Rockerbox, but the folding footrests themselves proved elusive. Plan A involved using the footrest part of the standard Triumph folding rear pillion footrests on the front hangers. The pivoting part of the footrest

was narrower than the 'slot', so I needed to retain the standard Thackeray washer to keep them steady. In addition the footrest 'drooped' slightly, so I had to build up the edge that bore against the hanger with a small amount of weld. This bodge seemed to work quite well, and looked authentic as well. However, the large Triumph footrest rubbers did not fit comfortably on the pillion rest, and the rests themselves were thinner than the standard ones and bit spindly.

So it was time for plan B. I set about the 'modified' footrests that came with the bike with an angle grinder to see if I could rescue the original footrests. One came out OK, but the other had suffered somewhat, both from the original welding up and my attempts to 'free' it. So it was back to the auto jumble circuit to find one footrest … One thing I did find out was that the bolt used to fit the T100C footrest was in fact a kick-starter pedal bolt, part number T1273/S541/S1971 (depending on which year's part book you use). Eventually, having failed to find a single footrest through the auto jumbles or spares dealers, I got the original one welded up and ground to shape at a local engineering firm. This cost £5, which was very reasonable considering I could not find a replacement anywhere. New footrest rubbers finished off the footrests.

The rear footrests that came with the bike were in pretty good shape, but I treated them to new Thackeray washers to try to stave off the dreaded 'Triumph rear footrest syndrome' – they always hang down except when brand new, which can be a pain if you need to make a quick engine start as the timing-side one obstructs the kick start swing. A coat of paint and new rubbers completed their renovation, and they could be bolted to the triangular stays that were in turn bolted to the rear sub frame.

The bike did not have a centre stand when I bought it, and I had been warned by the guys at Rockerbox that they were getting hard to find and were not cheap. So I was quite pleased when I found one at an auto jumble, freshly painted, apparently unbent and all for a mere £15. A fitting kit (bolts, nuts, tab washers and spring) was found on another stand. Actually fitting it to the

The centre stand gave some trouble when it was fitted. It was slightly twisted and was very stiff in operation. Easing the mounting flanges on the stand solved the problem.

bike was a bit of a struggle, as the new paint (so I thought) on both the stand and the frame made it a really tight fit. The stand was eventually persuaded to fit with some leverage and a bit of brute force and bolted into place. Once it was bolted on, the final job was to fit the return spring. The good news was that the top spring locating pin on the frame was easily accessible; the bad news was that the spring was incredibly strong.

There are three methods I use to fit stand springs, and all three of them usually result in a gashed hand or blood blister. Firstly I fitted the spring to the stand, and tried using a loop of electrical wire to pull the spring up and over its fitting on the frame. This failed when the wire broke, even when doubled up; luckily there was no damage to me, but it took a little time to find the spring, which had ricocheted off under the bench when the wire let go – I was surprised it did not hit me on its way like they usually do.

Plan B consisted of a raid on the family loose change jar, and collecting a large number of pennies. Then with the spring in the vice, I bent it over and put a penny in between each of the coils – trying to keep the pennies evenly spaced on each side to keep the spring straight. This plan also failed, as I could not get enough coins in the coils to stretch the spring long enough to slip it over both hooks – but then I did not get any fingers nipped by the coils when fitting so that was a plus point. Plan C was to revert to the 'official' way of doing it using a Phillips screwdriver to lever the spring up and over the frame fixing. I've tried this in the past and have had no success, so was astonished when it worked first time, resulting in the spring nestling on top of the frame lug, and needing just a tap from a hammer to get it properly seated. Fitting the stand took the best part of an afternoon, and if I was going to do it again, I would fit it to the frame before anything else to avoid grovelling on the floor so much! I had expected the stand to loosen off a bit once the powder coating was worn away with a bit of use, but this did not happen. Even the extremely strong return spring would not pull the stand up without assistance. Worse, even after putting the engine in, the stand was reluctant to come up, and the whole bike would skid along the garage floor. Something was definitely wrong, and I realized with a sinking feeling that I would have to remove it and sort the problem out. Getting the return spring off was awkward – I eventually levered it off with two screwdrivers. Close inspection showed that the flanges on the stand were not parallel. The immaculate and cheap stand was obviously cheap because it was slightly twisted. With some work on the grinder, I managed to get the flanges parallel and an easier fit into the frame flanges. On refitting, it went on very easily, in stark contrast to the first fit, and worked correctly. It even kept the front wheel off the ground as it was designed to, and the return spring even managed to pull the stand up when required. A quick fix had sorted what could have been a major problem.

The side stand that came with the bike was in good condition, but had a length of steel plate

For 1966 Triumph sent this T100SS onto the beach for a spot of relaxation.

welded to its foot. While the stand was fine, the fixing lug on the frame had been welded up in the past. It had probably been broken off at some stage, and was fairly crudely welded back on. The angle it was welded on at was wrong and made the bike lean over too far, and the stand did not tuck in far enough when folded up. The solution was to use an angle grinder to half cut through the welding, bend the lug to the correct position using the stand as a lever, then reweld the mounting lug in the correct position. I left the lump of steel plate on the stand as a reminder of the bike's history. On the first serious use of the side stand – when trying to start the bike at the end of the rebuild – my welding skills were exposed as wanting as the fixing lug, complete with stand fell off; my welding had not penetrated properly.

Front Forks Rebuild

The front forks that came with the bike were in one piece and complete. Inspection showed a few problems, such as a stripped thread in the han-

dlebar mount holes in the top yoke, but all the main bits were in good condition. The steering head bearings looked new, and had clean grease in them, and the stanchions were in good condition with no scoring or rust on the bearing surfaces, and they were straight. I decided to replace the fork leg bearings and obviously would be using new oil seals. The only unusable parts of the original forks were the seal holders, which were chromed but had suffered over the last thirty years and the chrome was rough and lifting. I have yet to find a chromer who can recover seal holders economically, and new ones are readily available and reasonably cheap. While I would have preferred to use stainless steel holders, only chromed ones were available at the time. Buying these from Rockerbox meant I could inspect them first, and get Arthur at Rockerbox to fit the oil seals – a job that needs a special tool and some skill to get right, as my collection of ruined seals testifies!

Restoring the top yoke presented some interesting problems. As well as the stripped thread in

The forks got new bushes and a good clean. The internals were reused, including the shuttle valves that provide two-way damping.

The top yoke during the rebuild, showing the headlamp fixing ears, the speedometer mounted on its bracket, and the stainless steel top nuts.

the handlebar lug, the steering lock needed some attention. The lock that came with the bike had no key, so had to be removed. This is easier said than done, as the lock assembly is retained with a countersunk grub screw that has its head concealed by a lead plug. The easiest way of getting the screw out is to drill into it using a small drill, straight through the lead plug, then unscrewing the grub screw using a square tapered rod hammered into the remains of the screw. I made up a new grub screw with a slot cut in its head to enable easier removal, without (hopefully) compromising security, and replaced the lock barrel with one that I had a key for. I also ran a tap down the handlebar clamp bolt holes to clean up the threads, realizing then that one was a stripped thread. A suitable helicoil thread insert was used to repair the thread, by tapping the hole out to a larger diameter and threading the helicoil 'spring' replacement thread into the hole then fixing it with locktight.

Once this work was done, I cleaned up the top yoke using a rotary wire brush and painted it black with the ubiquitous Smoothrite. The lower yoke was painted black as were the lower legs. The bike came with competition-type top shrouds, with no headlamp ears, so I ordered a set of new 1969 model year shrouds which had both headlamp ears and a lug to carry the ignition switch on the left-hand side. New bronze top and bottom bearings, stainless steel top and steering head nuts, and rubber gaiters completed the purchases, and enabled the assembly of an 'as new' set of forks. I rebuilt the fork legs first, using the new bushes and the existing stanchions.

I cleaned up the shuttle valves at the bottom of the stanchions and the fork sliders (lower legs), washing out all the old fork oil. With the new fork bushes fixed onto the stanchions, the new seal holders were screwed on using Triumph's special C-Spanner tool to wind them on. I used some silicon sealer on the threads to keep them oil tight – in the past I've used PTFE tape. With the fork legs completed, the springs and relevant steel and cork washers were assembled onto the top of the legs, the yokes were assembled into the frame (back from the painter's), reusing the exist-

ing ball bearings and cups, which were as new. I fitted the fork legs into the yokes using a home-made tool, comprising a 1ft-long (30cm) steel bar with a handle at one end and a turned-down top nut at the other. The tool is screwed into the fork leg, and then used to pull the stanchion up into the yokes against the pressure of the springs. With the legs in the yokes, the newly rebuilt front wheel could be fitted, and I had a rolling chassis.

Electrics

By 1969 Triumph (and BSA) had pretty much solved all the electrical gremlins that had haunted their models in the past. Moving to 12v increased reliability by halving the current (amps) needed to run the lights and ignition, while reliable semi-conductor voltage control using a Zener diode simplified the wiring loom. Alternator stators had their coils encapsulated in resin so they were better able to survive in the hot oily hell of the primary chain case, and a reasonably efficient rectifier converted the AC current to DC. The zener diode was mounted under the bottom yoke in an alloy finned bullet shaped heat sink, and the rectifier was positioned under the seat next to the battery. The ignition system by now used the individually adjustable Lucas 6ca points, which worked well, although the fibre heels could and did wear, making regular adjustment a requirement if correct ignition timing was to be maintained. Still, many of the electrical components have been superseded by more modern units, notably the ignition system with fit-and-forget magnetic triggering, and the regulating rectifying side of things being catered for with 'black boxes'. So I decided to take advantage of these advances when restoring the bike's electrics. My strategy was to keep the wiring as simple as possible while giving the bike a modern, up-to-date electrical system. I would depart from original in a number of ways by fitting:

• Indicators
• Electronic ignition
• Solid state combined regulator/rectifier
• New handlebar switchgear to control lights/

indicators/horn/headlight flasher
- A decent quartz halogen headlamp
- Front brake light switch

To this end, I did not take the simple option and just buy a new loom, as a standard Triumph loom would not meet my requirements, I decided to make my own loom following the standard Triumph wiring colours. This way I could tailor the loom both to the bike and the non-standard components fitted, rather than bodging extra wires into a standard loom.

As bought, the bike had a very sorry-looking rectifier and no Zener diode, heat sink or lights. This gave me a clean sheet to experiment. In the past I've used Zener diodes/rectifier systems, and have also used Podtronics solid state combined regulator/rectifiers. For this restoration, I decided to try a 'Sparx' combined regulator/rectifier. There were several reasons for this choice – I wanted to support a firm that was prepared to innovate and design new components that will not look out of place on a classic, take advantage of modern electronic technology, and test this type of technology. The neat thing about the Sparx unit is that it mimics the appearance of the Triumph Zener diode heat sink, and mounts in the same place on the bottom yoke in a nice cooling breeze. This struck me as being a very neat and elegant solution to updating the electrics but keeping it looking standard.

Lights were non-existent, which gave me a carte blanche to find front and rear fittings. In September 2006 I found a 6in (15cm) chromed headlamp from a 1971 BSA B25/Triumph T25 at the Netley Marsh auto jumble – at £20 it was cheaper than a new 6in painted shell, and also had the three warning lights (indicators, oil pressure and main beam) that I wanted. The only problem was the light switch that was fitted to these headlights – the Lucas type 31276, which was a rotary two-position unit giving side lights or main lights only, with the lights being turned on from the ignition switch. I wanted to use the standard three pole toggle switch used on the T100C (off, side lights, main lights – Lucas type 35710) but the hole left by the 1971-onwards switch was

larger than the diameter of the toggle switch. This meant I had to make up a stainless steel mounting washer on the lathe to adapt the toggle switch to fit in the larger hole in the headlamp shell. With the 'thin' fork yokes this headlamp was a tight fit in the new headlamp ears, but was persuaded to fit with a little force.

The rear light was another auto jumble find. Like the headlamp it was second hand, and compared to a new unit (£60) was very cheap at £20 – the same as the headlamp. It is a 1966 to 1967 model year rear light and probably the most stylish rear light ever fitted to a Triumph. The alloy casting is neat and shapely, and it carries a Lucas Type 679 light unit – aptly nicknamed the 'tit' rear light for obvious reasons. This unit fitted easily onto the rear mudguard, and only needed a couple of bullets soldered onto the wires to make it ready for connection.

New two-position ignition switches are readily available, and I procured one from Rockerbox. This was designed to be fitted into the housing in the left-hand side headlamp bracket, and only needed a pair of 90-degree spade connectors to fit it into the wiring loom.

I had decided to fit indicators to the bike as I am uncomfortable riding in modern traffic without them, so the handlebar switchgear needed to cater for this. There were several options for the handlebar switches – the cheap pressed tin switches of the type available in the late 1960s, the 1971 BSA/Triumph switch blocks, a Triumph Trophy Trail/Adventurer switch block (which was actually a Yamaha item) or the 1973 Triumph left-hand handlebar switch. I decided on the last option as the switch block gives dip/main light, indicators, horn and headlight flash (all I needed) and it was being re-manufactured by Sparx so was readily available. I had also used one on my BSA A65, and it has been robust and reliable over three years. While a Trophy Trail/Adventurer switch block (the Yamaha unit) would have been nice, I have never actually seen one in the flesh. No doubt lots will appear at the auto jumble after I've bought the Sparx item! One good trick is to use a Japanese flasher unit from a scooter – these are two-wire fitting, and

The Sparx combined regulator and rectifier looks like the original Zener diode heat sink, and it fits in the same place, under the headlamp. This gives it a good stream of cooling air, and saves having to find another mounting place.

are not too sensitive to the bulbs used in the flashers. Lucas three-wire flasher units can be very sensitive to the wattage of the flasher bulbs and will often not work if the 'wrong' 21-watt bulbs are used.

Sparx also produce an electronic ignition kit that includes the ignition coils, magnetic trigger mechanism and a control box that provides a progressive advance curve. As I needed new coils, and this kit was attractively priced and looked to be pretty good quality, I added it to my shopping list. Having assembled the components, all I needed to do was join them up with wire! I used modern Thinwall cable from Vehicle Wiring Products. This wire is a multi-strand copper high performance cable which uses thin high-performance hard grade PVC insulation, and is now the wire of choice for many motorcycle and car manufacturers. The cable is about two-thirds the diameter of the original specification cable for the same load-carrying capacity, so makes for a lighter but stronger loom, and is especially useful in areas such as the headlamp where there is not a lot of room in the first place. The only down side of the cable is it looks a bit skinny when compared to the old type of thick-wall cable.

To build the loom, I used the bike itself as a jig, and building up individual sections or circuits of the loom one at a time. These circuits were the main feed to the ignition switch with two power tails, one to the headlamp, one just off the switch, the ignition circuit, the indicators, lights and ancillaries (such as the oil pressure warning circuit and the front and rear brake light).

Each circuit was wired using the colour coding for the home-market post frame/engine

Wiring the bike to the 1971 specification led to to a very full headlamp! Luckily everything fitted eventually.

number KE00001, which had the indicators in the diagram. Interestingly, while using this 'standard' Triumph wiring diagram, I found two errors – the stop and tail light leads were transposed, and the main beam itself was marked up as the main beam warning light. This led to some head scratching and swapping around of wires!

My basic mode of operation was to take one circuit (that is, a connection between two points or components), then offer the wire (of the right colour code) to the two components that it was connecting, cut the wire roughly to length, and then solder an appropriate fitting (either bullet or spade) to one end. The wire could then be fixed it to that component, and then offered up to the component at the other end, trimmed to length, leaving a few centimetres to allow for flexing, and the relevant fixing soldered on the other end. If the fixings are spades, then you must make sure the correct sleeve is fitted over the wire before soldering the second spade on, as it is really difficult to fit the insulating cover after the event! While spade fittings can be crimped, I prefer to

crimp and solder the spades to the wire to ensure a good electrical and mechanical joint. The bullets I use are the traditional tinned brass types, which have to be soldered to the wire.

I made sure I left enough free cable to allow for fork movement around the steering head and also made up an additional earth wire to run into the headlamp. While running the earth through the steering head bearings was standard on older British bikes, it was not ideal and a separate earth should enable the front light's potential to literally shine out!

Once a circuit was complete, I would use a multimeter and check it all worked before moving on to the next one. Eventually, the bike was draped in wire and looking rather strange, but all of the circuits worked and there did not seem to be any duff earths or strange effect. Once all of the circuits were complete, I tidied up the loom by binding the loose wires in non-adhesive self-amalgamating PVC tape – making sure all holes that the wires went through had rubber grommets in them, and there was nothing else to add to the loom. The complete loom was then fixed onto the bike using cable ties onto the frame. The only bits that were not completed at this stage were the connections from the loom to the engine – the alternator to regulator circuit and the ignition trigger unit to ignition black box. These were left loose, and were completed once the engine was installed.

The only problem I had was with clearances within the small 6in (15cm) headlamp. The Lucas toggle switch was a lot deeper than the rotary switch, and the terminals were a bit tight against the light unit – but judicious positioning of the wires and some bending of the terminal blades gave enough room. The scooter flasher unit was also bigger than the Lucas unit and needed to be pushed well to the back of the shell to avoid any conflicts.

Engine and Gearbox

As bought, the engine had its head off and the primary drive dismantled and in a box. This is not ideal, but such is life when buying basket cases. At

The tops of the original pistons showed enough damage to warrant replacement. Luckily they were standard size, and the barrels did not need a re-bore.

least I could inspect the primary drive components, which seemed to be in reasonable condition. The pistons were standard but had some interesting witness marks on their crowns – which could have been where someone had been using a hammer on them, or, as an engineer friend suggested, they were evidence of flame erosion.

With no primary drive, it was difficult to turn the engine over, but pushing on the pistons gave some movement. There was no apparent play on the drive-side main bearing.

While preparing to strip the engine down I found a potential problem that could have been disastrous. The oil feed and return pipes run underneath the engine and are vulnerable if the engine is out of the frame. In this case, the oil retun pipe had been crushed, which could have had led to oil starvation.

I removed the timing case and tried turning the engine over using a spanner on the timing pinion nut. This worked, but the engine did feel stiff. The gearbox seemed fine, with all the gears present, the gear selection felt OK and the whole

thing seemed to be smooth to turn over, with no graunching, clicks or play on the main shaft. The gear train that drives the camshafts and the oil pump were all in good condition.

In summary, the gearbox seemed fine, the primary drive was also in pretty good condition, but the engine was stiff, and the pistons definitely needed replacement. So the engine needed to be stripped to allow me to replace the pistons and check the bottom end.

The first job was to take off the barrels, which were held onto the crankcases with eight special – and pretty tight! – twelve-pointed nuts. The gasket looked original. There was no wear on the tappets, so I removed them from the guide blocks and marked them individually to ensure they went back into the right hole on reassembly. The barrels even on these late models still have the indentation to clear the distributor cast into the fins – evidence of the Triumph 'it it ain't broke, don't fix it' philosophy.

Inspecting the barrels for wear showed no gouges or other evidence of mechanical mayhem, and measuring then showed they were

The traditional Triumph timing side exposed. Fore and aft cams are driven by gears from the crankshaft pinion, with the plunger oil pump run using a sliding block off the inlet camshaft.

Despite the engine losing the distributor in the early 1960s, the casting lug was never removed from the dies, and the barrels retained the cutaway in the fins to accommodate it.

standard (that is, they had not been re-bored) and were well within specification (68.98–68.99mm) and still round so did not need a re-bore. Armed with this knowledge, I went online and eBay came to the rescue with a set of genuine Meriden Triumph standard pistons at a very reasonable price.

When I took the barrels off, the old pistons were revealed, along with the piston rings. All seemed OK with little blow-by (brown staining on the pistons), which tended to confirm that the barrels were still well within specification. The pistons were removed, and access was gained to the con rods and crank. While the drive-side rod's big end bearing was good, with no play and free to move, the timing-side one was virtually seized onto the crank – this explained the stiffness felt when turning the engine over.

A word of caution here – with the barrels off the con rods can come into contact with the crankcase mouth, resulting in nicks or scratches in the rods. Triumph rods are highly polished to get rid of any surface imperfections that could result in stress cracks and failure of the rod. So the rods need to be protected from damage by wrapping some material (such as cardboard or plastic packaging) around the rod, and making sure they don't get scratched. If there are minor scratches or nicks in the rod, you can polish them out using very fine emery or metal polish. If they get deeply marked then consider changing them, as a broken rod will most likely destroy the barrels and crankcases – especially as rods tend to let go at high revs…

The stiff rod definitely meant that the crankcases would have to be split and the crank potentially reground. In any case, with a Triumph twin engine, if you do not know its history it is vital to clean out the sludge trap in the crank. Essentially the sludge trap (or 'crankshaft oilway', as Triumph describe it) comprises a large gallery or drilling in the crankshaft through the middle of the crank pins. Oil is fed under pressure into an inner oil tube in the gallery, and escapes through holes into the outside of the tube, hopefully leaving any sludge and other debris in the tube, where it is forced onto the inside walls of the tube by centrifugal force before it reaches the vulnerable soft metal of the big end bearing shells. An integral part of the oil filtration system, the oil tube will eventually fill up with sludge, cutting down the oil supply to the big ends. Hence it is vital to clean out the sludge trap.

In order to split the cases to get the crank out, the primary drive has to be dismantled (all done already!) and the timing-side pinion taken off.

The timing-side pinion is held on with a normally (right-handed) threaded nut, which on this engine just would not budge. It is usally best to loosen it off before removing the engine from the bike, so you can lock the engine and gearbox up using the rear wheel brake. In this case it was difficult to lock up the engine, so I took the brutal route and cut the nut off the crank with a cold chisel, making sure that I did not do any collateral damage to the pinion below. With the nut off, I removed the crankshaft pinion with the appropriate Triumph tool. You must use this tool as the pinion is hard but brittle (like most gears) and does not take kindly to being levered off; it is also a very tight fit on the crankshaft, but the right tool turns what can be a major pain into an easy job.

The gearbox outer cover came off with little effort; the kick start lever had to be removed, but the gear leaver could be left on, as its mechanism is fixed to the inside of the outer cover. After undoing the outer screws and two nuts, I could use the gear lever to pull off the cover. The inner cover was secured by two further screws, which in this case showed evidence of previous abuse in the shape of butchered heads. Also, just outside the top right-hand side of the cover was a crankcase stud, which needed either a very slim box spanner or the inner cover removed to get to it.

The workshop manuals for the bike gave differing advice as to whether the main shaft nut needed to be undone to remove the gear cluster – the earlier ones said no, the later ones said yes, so I removed it anyway, locking up the main shaft with an alloy rod against the final drive sprocket. The inner cover and gear cluster could then be

The gear cluster was in good condition. Note the 'W R' stamped on the gearbox inner cover denoting a 'wide ratio' box.

removed in one piece by tapping on the clutch end of the main shaft.

With the gearbox out of the way, the crank could be split. There are various studs holding the cases together around the periphery, some of which double up to hold the front engine plates, and most importantly there are two screws that fit in the crankcase mouth. If you don't remove these screws before trying to split the crankcases you run the risk of breaking the cases around the screws – rendering them to scrap! So don't forget to take them out.

The cases came apart easily – a few light taps on the outside of the cases with a wooden or plastic mallet encouraged the first signs of movement, and gentle wiggling then got the cases apart. Note that you don't need to remove the camshafts to split the cases.

The freed crankshaft, still with the connecting rods attached, came out of the crankcases easily. The rods were removed and the big end shells inspected. Both showed significant wear with the timing-side ('stiff') one showing significant ridges and damage, so it looked as if that big end had seized or partially seized – possibly the reason for the bike being taken off the road.

There were no obvious reasons for the seizure: the oil pump was fine, there were no metallic bits in the sump, and there was no blockage in the crank or oil ways. Checking for blockages is easily done using a pump action oil can – push it against an oil hole in the crank or cases and pump, and oil will come out somewhere. If it does not, then it is fairly obvious that the oil way is blocked!

Carrying out this operation on the crank resulted in dirty oil coming out of both big end journals – indicating that there was sludge present in the trap. The crank's timing side big end had been slightly scored as a result of the big end going, and needed to be measured up. So it was packed off to Rockerbox for checking and to have the sludge trap cleaned out. The sludge trap is retained by a screw-in plug with a slot for a screwdriver to unscrew it. Invariably, the plug is a pig to get out and usually has to be destroyed by drilling before it decides to move. Rockerbox do a retaining plug which is screwed in or out with an allen key, making future removal much easier. However, they were out of stock of them at the time, so a standard slotted plug was used. The crank's big end journals needed to be ground and were taken back to 10 thou undersize.

I could now clean up the cases and check over the gearbox while waiting for the crank to come back. Internally the gearbox casing was like new, all the gears were fine and the cam plate and selector forks were unworn. The only slightly worrying sign was the black sludge in the bottom of the box – but I guess that this was due to the bike having been left standing for a while.

The 'C' Series Triumphs, in common with other Triumphs and BSAs of the time, had a relatively complex arrangement to manage the oil level. There was a conventional filler plug on the top of the casing, and a drain plug on the underside. The drain plug was of a relatively large diameter, and had a concentric hole in it, sealed at the bottom with a small secondary bolt and washer, and had an open tube projecting up into the gearbox. The length of this tube was set to be at the correct level for the gearbox. The objective was to fill the gearbox with the drain

There are two screws on the inside of the crankcase mouth, pointed to here with the screwdriver. Failure to remove these screws will result in broken crankcases.

The gearbox level plug mechanism used in both Triumphs and BSAs was prone to giving wrong readings. Note how the gearbox oil level comes up to the middle of the bearings.

The damage to the primary chain case was not uncommon, and was caused by over-tightening the drain plug. Welding is the only solution.

plug in place, but with the small secondary plug left out. Once oil started to dribble out of the centre hole, the oil level was correct and the centre secondary plug could be replaced. This was all very well, but there was a problem. While many owners would not bother with the gearbox oil level, a diligent owner who checked the gearbox oil regularly could end up inadvertently draining the gearbox oil. Each time the level was checked, oil in the tube would dribble out – indicating to the owner the oil level was slightly over level. However, what was actually happening was that the oil was flung into the tube by the action of the gears whizzing around. So there was always oil in the tube, which the diligent owner was draining off each time the level was checked. The end result would be low gearbox oil despite the indicator showing that the level was correct (or slightly over).

Use of a toothbrush, white spirit and some elbow grease had the cases looking good.

The barrel was in good condition, with the bores still standard and within specification, and no broken fins. The silver paint on the barrels was past its best, so I set about them with a wire brush to get as much of the old paint and rust off as possible, then, after masking off the tappet blocks, spray-painted them with Finnigan's silver

Smoothrite. The first attempt was a disaster – I had not cleaned the barrels up sufficiently, and they ended up looking a real mess. So it needed paint stripper, a lot more elbow grease and more care to get them looking all right.

New pistons were required due to the damage to the tops of the originals, and again eBay came up with the necessary goods – a set of standard ex-Meriden pistons, complete with rings, gudgeon pin and circlips at a very reasonable price. Often with older engines there is a build-up of old instant gasket and other rubbish in the screw holes. To deal with this I grind down one side of an old casing screw, then screw it into all the holes. This lets the gunge out of the hole up the side of the screw and also identifies if there is any thread damage that need repairing. Luckily there were no damaged threads, and not a lot of gunge either.

The primary chain case looked to be in reasonable condition, but benefited from a bit of polishing to bring up a shine. Closer inspection revealed a crack around the drain plug (which also gives access to the primary chain adjuster). When the drain plug was screwed in it was apparent that the bottom half of the hole was almost separate from the rest of the case. In fact, it took very little effort to completely remove the lower 'run' of the hole, threads and all.

This is a relatively common fault, caused by over-tightening of the drain plug. The solution was to get the resulting damage alloy welded, and then re-drill a new hole and tap the appropriate threat to accept the drain plug.

Rebuilding the Engine

Rebuilding the engine was straightforward. The refurbished crank was supplied with new big end bearing shells, and I bought new main bearings. Fitting the new main bearings was surprisingly easy – I popped the cases in the oven at 150°C (300°F) for ten minutes, after which the old bearings came out simply with a light tap on the bench. The new bearings had been put in the freezer overnight, and these were then just dropped into the still warm cases. Once everything had cooled down and warmed up, they were a lovely tight fit in the cases. I fitted the new big end shells into the rods, and bolted them onto the crank, after making sure there was plenty of oil on the shells and journal. Then fitting the crank was simply a matter of offering it up to the cases, and bolting the cases together. The only tricky bit was making sure that the rotary breather valve was correctly positioned. I achieved this by sticking it and its spring on the end of the inlet camshaft using a good dollop of grease, before fitting the cases together. This ensured that the rotary valve was engaged in the slots in the camshaft.

Rebuilding the timing side was straightforward, re-timing the camshafts and bolting in the oil pump. With two new oil seals fitted to the timing cover, one for the crank end oil feed and one for the points compartment, the timing cover was fitted to the engine with new allen screws.

With the cases back together and the engine on the bench it was a simple matter to fit the new pistons to the rods, and fit the barrels. I use simple steel ring compressors, and tilted the engine on to its front to fit the cylinder block single-handed. Doing it this way means that the cylinder block can be rested on the bench, giving much better control of the operation and mini-mizing the possibility of breaking a ring. With a new cylinder base gasket and the eight 'star' nuts fitted and tightened, the bottom half of the engine was complete and there was no possibility of damaging the con rods or dropping anything inside the crankcases!

The Gearbox

With the engine completed, it was time for the gearbox. When I dismantled it there little or no wear and the black sludge in the case was easily cleaned out. In order to fit the gear cluster, I built it up on the bench into the inner cover, including the cam plate and selectors, then offered it up to the main case and slotted it home. However, when the inner casing was screwed up, the box locked up. This was a bit puzzling as the box had seemed all right when it was dismantled, but clearly something was not right. I eventually had to dismantle the cluster and inspected both the shafts, which seemed fine. I then took a close look at the bearings in the main casings (needle for the lay shaft and ball for the main shaft) and they were both fine as well. I had loosened the main shaft nut when I dismantled the engine, and thought that the main shaft might not be seating proper-ly in the bearing, but fitting the gearbox without the lay shaft showed no problem.

This implied the trouble was with the lay shaft, and the problem emerged when I took a close look inside the kick starter spindle, which carries the timing-side end of the lay shaft. The needle roller bearing had been disturbed, and several nee-dles had fallen out of the bearing and were lying loose in the inner recesses of the spindle. These loose needles were holding the lay shaft out slight-ly, causing it to lock up when the inner case was tightened down onto the gearbox casing. Remov-ing the old bearing was difficult, as it sat in a blind hole and there was no way to put a puller on it. After removing the remaining needles, I used a mini grinder to cut a groove in the remaining case, and then using a punch and chisel manged to collapse the side of the bearing enough to get a purchase on it and pull it out. A replacement was simply pressed in using the vice. With the new bearing installed, the gearbox could be reassem-bled into the inner casing, and then it was an easy job to slot it back into the main casing – I'd had plenty of practice by then! With the two inner screws (new allen screws to replace the butchered originals) tightened down, the gearbox operated correctly, and turned easily. The gearbox outer cover, with the undisturbed selector mechanism still attached, simply slotted on, and the gearbox was complete, with all four gears and neutral present. With the timing side of the engine complete, I could turn my attention to the drive side.

Drive Side

When I picked up the bike, the drive side had been dismantled and was in a box. I was pleasantly surprised that almost everything was present: primary chain, clutch, drive sprocket, alternator studs and the primary chain adjuster. The only major component missing was the complete alternator, but I was planning to buy a new one anyway – a thirty-year-old Lucas Stator and rotor would be feeling its age! Sparx came up with a new replacement. New clutch roller bearings were fitted, and the primary drive built. I had to get a new clutch hub, as the one that came with the bike had a chunk out of it on the rim, presumably where someone had levered it off rather than using the proper extractor. The important points here are to fit the primary chain adjuster before putting the alternator stator on, and to check the air gap between the rotor and stator.

Cylinder Head

With the bottom end substantially complete, it was time to turn to the cylinder head. The item that came with the bike was an earlier version, which meant there would be challenges with getting the right pushrod tubes. Earlier heads had two small holes to 'guide' the pushrods while later heads dispensed with these holes, leaving a larger single hole which the later, 'castellated' push rod tubes fitted completely, helping to reduce (note I'm not saying eliminate) oil leaks. In addition, the rocker boxes that I had were in pretty bad shape, needing a good recondition. Close inspection of the rocker boxes showed that on both the threads in the front fixings were shot, and in one the holes for the studs were grossly enlarged, and

there was half a stud still embedded. So on my auto jumbling list went a pair of replacements, with special emphasis on the condition of the front fixing studs. Kempton turned up a single bare new casting, and a couple of worn second-hand examples. In the end I used the new casting with the spindles and rockers from one of the old boxes, chose the best remaining one, and re-drilled and helicoiled the front stud holes. This box also needed its joint face cleaning up extensively, which I did using a sheet of emery paper on a piece of plate glass. With new rubber seals on the rocker shafts and allen key type adjusters, the rocker boxes were fit for service.

As I had no push rod tubes, I bought a pair of early ones to match the head. However, these did not fit over the late tappet blacks that were fitted to the 1969 on models, which were a larger diameter to accommodate the later push rod sealing arrangement. I ended up replacing the later tappet blocks with earlier versions, which meant removing the barrels I had fitted earlier. However, the replacements were fitted reasonably easily using a proper Triumph tappet block tool to drive out the old ones and drive in the new ones. The only difficulty was in making sure the new blocks were driven in square so the little locating bolt could be fitted properly. The barrels were then refitted and the engine was carefully dropped into the frame, avoiding scratching the powder coating on the frame.

With the head off, the engine went into the frame easily and I slipped the bottom fixing stud so the engine could rock forwards and backwards. I then had some problems with lining up the rear engine plates. On inspecting the parts manual, I found they were handled, with a cut out on the timing side to accommodate the gearbox housing. I'd put them on the wrong way round of course, so had to dismantle them from the frame (and the assorted oil tank and mudguard brackets) in order to switch them. Once that was done, they slotted into place, and I loosely fitted the front engine plates.

With the engine in the frame, I could fit the push rod tubes to the tappet blocks with new seals and a light smear of silicone gasket. The top

The drive side of the restored T100C shows the new exhaust pipes and the clean lines of the bike.

push rod tube seals were fitted to the head, again with a light smear of sealant. It was time to prepare the head gasket. I used the standard solid copper one, but even though it was new I annealed it on the gas hob – heating it until it was glowing cherry red and then dropping it into cold water. This makes the gasket soft, and hence it should give a good, gas-tight seal when the head is bolted down.

With the head sitting loosely on top of the barrel and gasket and push rod tubes, I was able to slot in the push rods through the holes in the head. Fitting new rocker box gaskets meant that the rocker boxes could be placed on top of the head. With the engine loose in the frame, the four inside head bolts that also fix the rocker boxes in place could be fitted by rocking the engine sideways so the studs cleared the top tube of the frame. The four outer head bolts were screwed

into place and the head was tightened down. At this point it pays to make sure the valve gear is working properly by turning the engine over. One of the inlet valves was not moving, as its push rod had not properly engaged on the tappet – so it was off with the rocker box and a quick fiddle to get the rod in place.

With everything looking good, I torqued down the eight head studs, and then fitted the various screws and nuts that fixed the edges of the rocker boxes onto the head. The tappets were adjusted to specification (0.002 inch (2 thou or 0.05mm) inlet, 0.004 inch (4 thou or 0.10mm) exhaust) using the allen key adjusters, and the head was finished off with a set of new tappet covers. These were the later pattern type with the threads machined off at the top of the cover to take a rubber seal – this both helps to secure them in place and stops any leaks.

ABOVE: *The finished bike, looking good with the newly painted tank, new seat and exhaust system.*
BELOW: *The author astride the finished T100C.*

Exhaust

With the engine bolts tightened up, it was time to see about fitting the exhaust system.

On the 'C' Series engines up to 1972, the exhaust pipes fit over steel stubs that screw into the head, and are fixed in place using finned clamps. On the 1969 T100C the exhaust system is high-level, and both pipes sweep over the top of the primary chain case and are fixed in place with a vertical bracket that connects to the rear brake pedal stop on the frame. The pipes are joined together at the end of their run with a chromed H-piece. The silencers then fit onto the other ends of the H-piece and are supported from a bracket that fixes to the rear footrest bracket and the top of the seat stay, just below the shock absorber mount. A large wire grille (known as the 'chip basket' in the UK and the 'barbeque grill' in the US – a reflection on our different cultures!) shields the rider's and passenger's legs from the hot exhaust, and this is fitted with two clips. All of these different components tend to fit together somewhat randomly, and it took several tries before the pipes were in place and looking correct. However, a couple of hours' work, several skimmed knuckles and expedient use of a plastic mallet eventually had the system on and securely fixed in place! And what a difference it made – the system really did (and still does) look spectacular.

It was time to start her up – but there was a problem. After lots of kicks, the bike was not showing any signs of life. The carburettor did catch fire a couple of times when the bike spat back, but a swift bit of blowing put the flames out with no damage – it is always a good idea to have a fire extinguisher ready just in case when trying to start a newly rebuilt bike! With the bike refusing to go, I tried altering the timing from the initial settings given by the Sparx electroinic ignition, but this made no difference – it just would not start. I was convinced it was an electrical issue, but eventually checked the compression. It was well down on one side, so I had to take the head off to find out what was wrong.

As mentioned previously, the cylinder head that was supplied with the bike was an early T100 type. There are two distinct types of head used on the later 500cc bikes. Both have hemi-

spherical combustion chambers (unlike the early type 'squish band') but differ in the type of push rod tube and seals. The early type (up to 1968) used the shorter parallel-sided tubes, which had silicon rubber seals top and bottom; this head had two small holes at each end to 'guide' the push rods up to the rockers. The later head was redesigned to try to make the push rod tubes oil-tight, and used push rod tubes that were 'castellated' and intruded into the head, so there was a large hole at each end of the head that positively located the tube and its seal in the head. These push rod tubes were widened at their base, and the tappet blocks were wider to allow for an internal O-ring seal, again giving more positive location and better sealing.

In order to fit the earlier head I had to use the early push rod tubes, and to accommodate these I had to replace the tappet blocks in the barrel. Removing the head, I put the head springs side down on the bench and filed both combustion chambers with oil. The timing-side chamber emptied a lot quicker than the drive side, confirming that the compression problem was to do with the valves. Close inspection of the valve seats showed a small but obviously significant amount of damage to the valve seat, which was too deep to grind out. Luckily I found a new head (as in new old stock) on eBay, and bought it. This was quicker than getting the old head refurbished, and meant that I now had the correct head for the 1969 bike – but this meant changing the old type tappet blocks for the later type, and sourcing a set of late-type push rod tubes.

With these components bolted back onto the bike, and the exhaust system reinstalled, the bike burst into life after several kicks. It was ready for fine tuning and then off down to the local MoT testing station to start the process of getting it on the road. I trailered the bike down to my local test station. Although it is perfectly legal to ride an unregistered bike to an MoT test, as long as it is insured, I did not want the hassle of explaining this to the police if they did stop me! The bike passed the MoT with no problems, and then it was off up to the local DVLA office to get the bike registered.

Registering a Newly Rebuilt Bike

In the UK, if you buy a bike that is unregistered and you cannot find out what the original registration number (if any) was, then you need to get it a registration number before you can ride and enjoy it.

If you present a vehicle to the Driver and Vehicle Licensing Agency (DVLA) for registration, then there are two things that can happen. The bike can be given an 'age-related' number or a 'Q' plate. In order to get an age-related plate, you must supply a dating certificate that states the year of manufacture of the bike. These are available from clubs or from independent consultants who advertise in the classic bike press. A historic plate should result in up to 1962 bikes getting a registration number in 'ABC123' format, while 1962-onwards bike would get a age related letter at the end of the number, for example 'ABC123A'. The number awarded is non-transferable, so it cannot be sold on to a number plate dealer to be put onto another bike or car. When the age of a vehicle cannot be accurately determined, a 'Q' plate with the format 'Q123ABC' is used.

In order to apply for a 'new' registration document, there is a set of data that needs to be supplied to the DVLA. The main form needed is the V55/5, which, to quote the DVLA, 'is used by independent dealers, import dealers and individuals to register brand new vehicles, new and used imported vehicles, kit built vehicles, rebuilt vehicles and used vehicles not previously registered at DVLA.'

A new registration number will only be issued to a roadworthy vehicle, as the registration process includes the issue of a Road Fund Licence, or tax disc. In order to get a tax disc, you must have a valid MOT test certificate and insurance, so you have to get the bike ready for the road before it can be registered.

Getting hold of a V55/5 can prove slightly problematic. They are available from the DVLA and DVLA local offices, but if you do not want to travel up to your local office (my local office, for example, is in Reading, some 20 miles/32km away) then you will need to contact the DVLA directly. The V55/5 is not available electronically from the DVLA website (www.dvla.gov.uk), where a number of other forms are available for downloading. You will need to telephone the DVLA (0870 240 0010) and once you have worked through the rather convoluted automated call system, talk to a person and request that a V55/5 be posted to you. This form identifies the additional information that needs to be provided.

Assembling the Information

In order to get a historic registration number, you will need to pull together a range of supporting information and data. As well as the V55/5 application form, I needed:
• Dating certificate – supplied from a DVLA approved source and will identify the frame and engine numbers and the date of manufacture. The certificate provides the DVLA with the date of the vehicle from an independent and approved source. Rubbings of the frame and engine numbers may be needed before a certificate can be issued.
• MOT certificate – once the restoration is complete the bike needs be MOT tested to ensure it is roadworthy before a registration number and tax disc is issued. It is legal to ride a bike without a registration number to a pre-booked MOT test, or trailer the bike over to the MOT test station. If you ride the bike it must be insured.
• Insurance certificate – you will need to get the bike insured before applying for a registration number. As you have not got a registration number, the bike needs to be insured on the basis of the frame number, and this did not pose a problem with my current insurer (Carole Nash). However, the road aspect of the insurance is valid for only a limited period, in my case four weeks, after which the insurance reverts to fire and theft only. Once you get the registration number the road aspect can be reinstated by calling the insurer with the new registration number.
• Identification documents – in order to register a machine, you must provide evidence of your identification. A photocard driving licence is acceptable, but if you don't have one, then you must provide one of: old-style paper licence, passport, marriage certificate, decree nisi/absolute certificate or birth certificate, and proof of your address as entered on the V55/5 (one of: utility bill, bank/building society statement, medical card or council tax bill for the current year).

Finally you have to pay a fee for the registration (this was £50 in 2007), and if applicable pay the cost of the Road Fund Licence. In 2007, if a bike was built before 1973, its tax class is 'Historic Vehicle', so the Road Fund Licence fee is zero.

Formal Inspection

Once you have assembled all of the evidence and have a filled in V55/5, you will need to visit your DVLA local office. Presenting the V55/5 and the supporting evidence

The author astride the finished T100C.

(including the fee), you may be issued with an age-related number there or then or the staff may need an independent inspection carried out. The office staff will verify your identification using the required documents described above, and then check that the V55/5 is correctly filled in and that the supporting evidence is correct. They will take the V55/5, MOT certificate, dating certificate and insurance certificate and the £50 fee, issue you with a tracking reference number and tell you that you should get a reply soon. In a couple of days to a week you should be informed by letter if the vehicle needs inspection, and, if so the letter should contain details of the time and place for the inspection, which usually is the nearest VOSA testing station. So on the appointed day, you need to get the bike to the site.

Once there, the VOSA people should be expecting you, and the DVLA inspector will examine the bike. He will check the frame and engine numbers and verify that they match those on the V55/5, and may also take a look at any receipts, both from the original vendor of the wreck and some of the receipts from various parts suppliers. All in all the inspection process takes about fifteen minutes.

Now you have to sit back and wait. In my experience it takes one to two weeks to receive all of the documents back from the local office by post, which will include a new tax disc and a Number Plate Authorisation Certificate' (DVLA Form V948) which will tell you your new age-related number. The covering letter should state that a new V5C would be posted from DVLA in the next four weeks. You can get a registration number plate made up using the V948, and after reinstating the bike's insurance over the phone (if needed), you can at long last ride the bike on the road.

Summary

While you do have to jump through a number of hoops to get a bike registered in the UK, the process is fairly straightforward and seems to run quite smoothly. We all appreciate the need for proper identification of the vehicle owner, in line with the government's attempts to regain control of the registering of vehicles, and the requirement for an independent inspection, which makes it harder to re-register a stolen vehicle with an altered frame number. The only gripe I have is the time between applying for the registration and the appointment for the vehicle inspection. I suspect that this is governed by the availability of the inspector. It is frustrating to have completed the bike but not be able to put it on the road for another month. It's also a shame that you can't get the bike registered without an MOT certificate – if this was not needed then an application could be made at any time, the bike (or pile of bits) could be inspected and then the registration number awarded. The bike would still need to be subjected to an MOT test before it could hit the road, but then that is necessary anyway. However overall the process is straightforward and the system seems to be able to cope with classic bikes effectively.

Bibliography and Further Reading

Bacon, Roy, *Triumph – T90 and T100 Unit Twins* (Niton Publishing; ISBN 1-85648-308-8). Short Monograph on the sports 350cc and 500cc 'C' Series Twins.

Bacon, Roy, *Triumph Twins and Triples* (Osprey Publishing Ltd; ISBN 0-85045-403-4). Comprehensive history of the postwar Triumph twins and triples. Includes lists of engine and frame numbers and general specifications.

Brooke, Lindsay and Gaylin, David, *Triumph Motorcycles in America* (MBI Publishing Company; ISBN 0-87938-746-7. Well-researched and readable history of the Triumph marque in the USA.

Brooke, Lindsay, *Triumph Racing Motorcycles in America* (MBI Publishing Company; ISBN 0-7603-0174-3). An incredibly comprehensive book that covers Triumph's competition successes in the USA.

Clew, Jeff, *Turner's Triumphs* (Veloce Publishing Ltd; ISBN 1 901295-87-7). A definitive work on the life of Edward Turner by one of the most knowledgeable motorcycle writers. Includes the text of Turner's report on the Japanese industry.

Cycle World on Triumph 1962–1977 (Brooklands Books; ISBN 1-869826-574). A collection of road tests of Triumphs reprinted from the US magazine Cycle World. Contains a number of tests of 'C' Series twins, and includes a test of a Daytona-type racer.

Cycle World on Triumph 1967–1972 (Brooklands Books; ISBN 1-869826-582). A collection of road tests of Triumphs reprinted from the US magazine Cycle World. Contains a number of tests of 'C' Series twins and an informative article on the 350cc Triumph Bandit.

Davies, Ivor, *It's Easy on a Triumph* (Haynes; ISBN 0-85429-786-3). Ivor Davis was in charge of Triumph's advertising. This book comprises many pictures and anecdotes from his experiences working for Triumph, and contains a large number of detailed pictures of the 1973 ISDT TR5T.

Hartley, Peter, *The Ariel Story* (Ariel Owners Club, no ISBN). This history of the Ariel has a reference to the Ariel Impala, which was a Bandit/Fury engined prototype using an Ariel frame.

Hopwood, Bert, *Whatever Happened to the British Motorcycle Industry* (Haynes; ISBN 1 85960-427-7). The definitive account of the decline and fall of the industry told through the eyes of one of its most influential and talented engineers.

Nelson, J R, *Triumph Tiger 100 and Daytona* (Haynes Publishing; ISBN 1-85960-428-5). Written by an ex-Meriden man, the book covers all of the Tiger 100 models, pre-unit and unit, and the Daytona. Also available is a supplement to this volume that lists the part numbers used on the models year by year.

Wilson, Stephen, *British Motor Cycles, Volume 5* (Patrick Stephens Limited; ISBN 1-85260-021-7). This volume of Steve Wilson's incredibly comprehensive history of the British industry from 1950 to the 1980s covers the history of the Triumph Company.

Wilson, Stephen, *British Motor Cycles, Volume 6*, (Patrick Stephens Limited; ISBN 1-85260-392-5). This volume of Steve Wilson's history covers Triumph's bikes.

Woolridge, Harry, *The Triumph Speed Twin and Thunderbird Bible* (Veloce Publishing Ltd; ISBN 1-904788-26-2). Includes full specifications of the 'C' Series Speed Twin. Loads of detail and good illustrations.

Woolridge, Harry, *The Triumph Trophy Bible* (Veloce Publishing Ltd; ISBN 1-903706-12-2). Model by model coverage of the 1961–74 'C' Series Trophy offroad models including the Adventurer/Trophy Trail – written by an ex-Meriden man with extensive first-hand knowledge of the Triumph marque.

Recommended Suppliers

All of the following suppliers provided spares and advice to me during the rebuild, and I can thoroughly recommend them both in terms of the quality of goods supplied, and in the service provided to me. All the suppliers are based in UK (unless otherwise stated), and the telephone numbers are for the UK. International callers should replace the first 0 with 44.

Yeomans
Drayton Mill
Drayton
Nr Belbrougton
Worcestershire DY9 0BT
Tel 01562 730004
An excellent source of used spares, complete bikes and projects. Based in an old mill west of Birmingham, Yeomans is one of those shops that should have disappeared by now! It is a treasure trove of hard to find second-hand parts for many different mainly British marques.

Central Wheel Components Ltd
Wheel House
8/9 Station Road
Coleshill
Birmingham B46 1HT
Tel 01675 462264
Fax 01675 466412
www.central-wheel.co.uk
Suppliers of rims and spokes. A supplier I have used for all my restorations, and from whom I have always received prompt and knowledgeable service. Rims and spokes have always been of good quality, with a range of options such as 'ordinary' and 'better'-quality chrome rims, alloy rims and stainless steel rims. Also supply tyres and will build wheels.

Ebay
www.ebay.co.uk
A wonderful source of both spares and literature relating to classic bikes – and indeed classic bikes as well!

JR Technical Publications
Unit 3
Ladbrooke Park
Miller Road
Warwick CV34 5AE
Tel 01926 408844
Fax 01926 408866
www.triumph-spares.co.uk.
Purveyors of original and reproduction Triumph literature. They are officially licensed by the modern Triumph Motorcycles to supply official Triumph literature, including parts lists, workshop manuals and handbooks for most Meriden Triumph models. And their reproductions look just as they were in the 1960s and 70s.

Rockerbox
31 The Street
Wrecclesham
Farnham
Surrey GU10 4QS
Tel 01252 722973
Support my local motorcycle shop! Triumph spares and mechanical work. Get advice from Darrel, spannering by Arthur, tea by request. A traditional motorcycle shop, specializing in Triumph parts and complete bikes, but not averse to the odd BSA, Velocette or other British iron.

Tri-Cor

The Old Hopkiln
Whitwick Manor
Lower Eggleton
Ledbury
Herefordshire HR8 2UE
Tel/fax 01432 820752
www.tri-corengland.com

I have used Tri-Cor in the past, when they were called Rare Spares, while restoring my 1970 Bonneville and they provided excellent service then. It was a pleasure to return to them, albeit mainly by phone, and there were very few items I needed that they could not provide – and then they let me know over the phone. Orders were dispatched promptly and always contained what I had ordered. Tri-Cor also run Sparx, who manufacture various electrical components, including the Zener diode heat sink lookalike regulator/rectifier, T140 switchgear, and the electronic ignition that I used.

Vehicle Wiring Products

9 Buxton Court
Manners Industrial Estate
Ilkeston
Derbyshire DE7 8EF
Tel 0115 9305454
Fax 0115 9440101
Email sales@vehicleproducts.co.uk

I have used them for all my restorations, and have received consistently good service. Suppliers of everything you need to rewire a bike, such as bullet connectors, spade terminals and correctly colour-coded wire. They also do reproduction switches, lights, indicators and electrical fixtures, and some other motorcycle-related items such as control levers.

Index